ON THE ASHES

Release Worry, Guilt and Fear,
and Embrace the Calling of your Soul

KYLIE ZEAL

Copyright © 2019 Kylie Zeal
All rights reserved

ISBN: 978-0-9954041-2-0 (paperback)
ISBN: 978-0-9954041-9-9 (e-book)

The moral rights of the author have been asserted

All rights reserved. Except as permitted under the *Australian Copyright Act 1968* (for example, a fair dealing for the purposes of study, research, criticism or review), no part of this book may be reproduced, stored in a retrieval system, communicated or transmitted in any form or by any means without prior written permission.

All enquiries should be made to the author.

Text design by Charlotte Gelin
Cover design by Designerbility
Editing by Grammar Factory

A catalogue record for this book is available from the
National Library of Australia

 A catalogue record for this book is available from the National Library of Australia

Disclaimer

The material in this publication is of the nature of general comment only, and does not represent professional advice. It is not intended to provide specific guidance for particular circumstances and it should not be relied on as the basis for any decision to take action or not take action on any matter which it covers. Readers should obtain professional advice where appropriate, before making any such decision. To the maximum extent permitted by law, the author and publisher disclaim all responsibility and liability to any person, arising directly or indirectly from any person taking or not taking action based on the information in this publication.

For My Tribe

CONTENTS

DANCE ON THE ASHES	9
INTRODUCTION	11
REVIEWING	15
THE INDOCTRINATION	17
Evict Doubt	21
MINDSET VERSUS THE SYSTEM	23
Every Breath is an Opportunity	27
LIVING WITHIN THE SYSTEM	29
Outdated Rules	33
REALISING	37
POWER	39
You Are the Placebo	40
CONFUITION	41
Make Your Move	43
IT'S NOT OKAY TO LET PEOPLE DOWN, OR IS IT?	45
The Only Two People You Need to Impress	49
THE DEATH CLOCK	53
Do What is True for You	56
SOMETHING TO LOSE	57
Worry is Not Insurance	60
ANXIETMENT	63
Words are Like Keys	65

RECKONING 67

LOVE IS 69
Life Beset with Love Challenges 73
I CHOSE ME 77
Your Happiness is Your Responsibility 81
WHAT'S THE WORST THAT COULD HAPPEN? 83
Answer the Scary Questions 90
NO MONEY FOR THE RENT 93
Advice Converter 97
THE EVERYDAY GOOD STUFF 99
Focus 104
NO MORE BS 107
Faith Must Be Your Conviction 111

RELEASING 117

DROPPING THE WEIGHTS 119
Thoughts Have Weight 122
EMOTIONAL BAGGAGE REMOVAL 127
Forgive 131
ANY IDIOT CAN FALL IN LOVE 133
There is a Happily Ever After 137
LET IT BURN 141
You Were Born or Change 143
SOME DAYS 145
A Code of Conduct 149
THE SWEET SPOT 151
Your North Star 156

RISING 161

C.L.E.A.R. THINKING 163
Reveal 167
SILENCE IS MY HUSTLE 169
Be Silence 171
IT LOOKS THE SAME
BUT IT'S ACTUALLY DIFFERENT 173
The Higher You Go, the Better the View 177
MY EDITOR WAS SO ANNOYING 179
Life's Way of Making You Better 181
MY TRIBE 183
Empowered Women Empower Women 187
AN UNDENIABLE MELODY 191
Courageous and Outrageous 193

WORKS CITED 195

ACKNOWLEDGMENTS 197

ABOUT THE AUTHOR 199

DANCE ON THE ASHES

We will journey together. We will each take a brick and laying a path for the change that is coming.

Our love is fierce and our truth is real, and when our love and truth are repressed, it is the greatest source of our pain. But now, we will turn our pain into power.

There is a rumble in the ground. There is a collective heartbeat. There is choreography being taught and we will dance.

We will write down our fears and throw them in the fire. We will watch those fears rise with the smoke and disappear, and we will dance on the ashes.

INTRODUCTION

This book is a journey to empowerment.

Empowerment looks different for each person - but not that different. I've journeyed as a trusted guide with many people on their path to empowerment and I've become very familiar with the process and stages along the way. After a decade of coaching it's very clear, while the context in which the journey is travelled is usually unique to each person, the lessons and wisdom you must acquire to move further along the empowerment path are very similar.

You begin, as does this book, with **'reviewing'**. Something triggers you to start looking – to find the point in time where you ended up on the wrong path. Understanding why you continue to behave in ways that keep you disempowered. Or why you keep undervaluing yourself. You look way, way back and see that some causes have been around almost as long as you have, sometimes longer. You also see how a script was written for you and how you, often times, unquestioningly followed it.

As you continue to review, you begin **'realising'** where you gave your power away and, more concerningly, where you continue to give it away. This is no longer an appropriate or effective way to live if you want to create the life you envision for yourself and be happy. The realisation that your happiness is not only your right, but also your responsibility, becomes an undeniable truth.

You notice the ways you have let go of yourself in order to appease others. You begin to acknowledge all the ways you've been teaching others how to treat you. And as you feel your increasing resistance to external expectations and rules that keep you small, and dare to demand all the things your soul longs for, you find yourself at the **'reckoning'**. It's inevitable. In your new, empowered life, not everything can stay.

It won't always be easy to say no and let go, but it will be necessary in order to begin **'releasing'** that which is not aligned with your highest and healthiest vision for yourself. When you let go of that which is holding you back and weighing you down, you will sense your consciousness **'rising'**, and with it, your confidence, courage and certainty for who you are – an extraordinary, divine, empowered woman.

REVIEWING

THE INDOCTRINATION

It is a rare woman who does not lose her deep connection with her inner voice in the process of growing up. As a child, she has a strong connection to her inner world and imagination. But as she grows up, things change. The rules that society places on girls as they enter adolescence, on the verge of becoming women, is intense. The messages about expectations and compliance are delivered virtually non-stop and they create a racket. Trying to hear one's own voice amongst a sea of voices can be challenging.

It would be nice if we were like a bead of oil dropped into water. That drop of oil moves around with the water but it remains distinct from it. It is always clear where the water finishes and the oil begins. We are much more solvent than the oil. Once we are brought into the prevailing culture, we quickly dissolve, and it is virtually impossible to see where the culture ends and we begin.

As children, we are unaware we even need to maintain a concept of self, let alone any idea about how to achieve this difficult task so young. Instead, we do all that we can to satisfy our instinctive desire for acceptance and connection.

Girls have a very natural tendency towards relationships. We crave them. While we may express it in different ways, we are obsessed with relationships and love. We are highly emotional beings and our empathy and sensitivity are simply part of our natural compass. Of course, these are generalisations, and every female (and male) will vary. What doesn't change is that femininity is a strength – at least, it is until we grow up and undergo a process of indoctrination into a culture that would have us believe otherwise.

I became most uncomfortably aware of the indoctrination process while reading Carol Gilligan's book, *Joining the Resistance*. Gilligan wrote, 'It was the research with girls that elucidated more radically an intersection where psychological development collides with the demands of patriarchy, its gender norms and roles and values. The research highlighted what had previously been taken as a stage in the normal course of development and showed it to be a process of initiation, the induction of the psyche into patriarchy.'

Upon reviewing the research, my own indoctrination was quite apparent. While growing up, I, like so many of the girls in Gilligan's study, experienced feelings of 'losing my mind' or not being able to trust my own judgements. I too was caught up in the 'riddle of femininity' in patriarchy, which forces girls to choose between having a voice and having relationships.

As females, we have emotions, thoughts and feelings within us which clash with societal expectations. So we tend to separate these inner parts of ourselves and hide those parts that are not considered acceptable. We quiet our internal voice and keep it secret and away from judgement, in order to protect ourselves from being rejected by the culture we are moving into as young women.

As we become women we sense something is not right. Something is surely amiss when women are ridiculed, demonised or patronised for being women. When natural, life giving functions like breastfeeding or menstruation become excuses to shame women, something has gone awry. When women make up approximately half the world's population but significantly less of the governing institutions, something untoward is taking place.

As we review our history as well as our present, we also see examples of fierce women who rejected their indoctrination. Unfortunately, they often paid a high price for their defiance against systems attempting to enslave or defame them. But fortunately for us, their legacies live on as women who forced changes in spite of everything they were up against. Their victories, in spite of their losses, inspire us. Thanks to their courage, we can look at our own reflections and see what is possible.

EVICT DOUBT

Dear Sister, you are more intuitive than you know.

You have an internal guidance system more powerful than any technology. You were born with it. But, you know, sometimes this is the problem; when a gift is simply given, it is often taken for granted and not valued as much as it would be if it needed to be earned.

If you'd had to earn it, then perhaps you would have protected it more defiantly when external opinions tried to label you irrational. Instead, you let down your guard, and doubt simply walked in through the front door. Doubt then filled every room; there was no longer any place, even in your own home, where you were free from doubt.

Sister, how long are you going to let doubt live rent-free in your home?

It's time to evict doubt. Your intuition and doubt can no longer live together.

They were never good housemates to begin with. Intuition needs space in order to express her powerful insights. She needs somewhere she can completely be herself; where she can play the music as loudly as she wants, or have complete silence, or walk around naked. She needs a place of her own, free from doubt.

MINDSET VERSUS THE SYSTEM

Reviewing all the ways I had been indoctrinated into a system designed to keep me inferior left me feeling annoyed and resentful. I was frustrated by the injustice of the system, as well as all the time I wasted living by rules and expectations that didn't serve me.

What often gives me cause for concern is that I feel the injustice even though I'm privileged. I'm a white, heterosexual, educated woman with no disabilities. Life is really not that bad for me. Sure, there was that time that I was discriminated against because I was a woman. There are also daily expectations about how I should appear and speak. And there was that time that I was sexually assaulted – I had to put quite a lot of time and money into getting therapy for that. But, still, I know my life is not bad. I know many women and young girls have suffered much worse, and continue to suffer across the planet – and that makes me angry.

Rather than simply be angry, I think about how I can help make the world better. It sometimes feels too hard to fix big, systemic problems but I do my best to remember that every bit counts. If many people contribute to change, then there will be change. So then I consider my skills and work experience and how I can use them to make a positive difference.

I might not have grown up wealthy and I've certainly had challenges but, in the system I live in, I've also had more than enough opportunity to create wealth (emotional, physical, spiritual, mental and financial). I've still needed to work hard and apply a lot of discipline, live with integrity and develop an empowered mindset. But as long as I did those things, I'd be successful because I had resources available to me.

Interestingly, there are people who don't have privilege, who might not even have arms and legs, who have created great abundance for themselves. Without disregarding what inspiring and wonderful examples of success they are, I've noted they still had 'something' that enabled them to rise up.

Conversely, I once strongly advised a friend who was complaining about his lot in life: "You're a white, heterosexual male, over six feet tall, smart and good looking, and you live in a first world country. You have no good excuse for the poor situation you're in." But, actually, he didn't have that 'something' that enabled him to rise above his circumstances.

That 'something' is mindset. And attaining a mindset that raises a person up is easy and it's not. It's within your control and from that perspective, developing an empowering mindset is easy. But mindset is also heavily influenced by the system in which a person lives. So, even if changing mindset is easy, changing a system is not.

Systems take many, many years to develop. Take the patriarchy for example. That system has been instilling beliefs into malleable minds, both male and female, for centuries. Possible carriers of patriarchal beliefs include our parents, teachers and the government. They learned those beliefs from the people who came before them, and same for the people before them. It only takes a few generations before people are adhering to social norms they didn't create and, if they took the time to question, they might not even agree with them. But... it's just the way it's always been done. It's ingrained into the culture. And change tends to make people nervous – it makes some people so nervous and afraid, they are willing to judge and scold those who deviate from social rules.

I sometimes get really excited to be witnessing important changes in my lifetime; changes effectively dismantling the patriarchy. But it's also disheartening whenever we are fighting for the same things our grandmothers had to fight for. Frustrated, I cover my face with my hands and wrack my brain,

'Why does it have to be so hard? What's wrong with people?'

Then I pause and remember, 'it's the system'. Of course, that is no excuse for blatant sexism, domestic violence and rigid definitions of femininity and masculinity. But it does help me gain perspective and reminds me what we're really up against. It drives me to keep doing my work empowering others to be more confident, self-assured leaders – to contribute to the 'mindset' that will rise above, and then take down, an unjust and unsustainable system.

EVERY BREATH IS AN OPPORTUNITY

Dear Sister, your story was started before you were born.

Your home, your heritage, your name. It was laid out, waiting for you to fulfil your role.

It was not necessarily that anyone wanted to confine you. Though they may, even innocently, have done just that.

Regardless, the story is not over. Every breath is an opportunity to rewrite the ending.

LIVING WITHIN THE SYSTEM

When I was twenty-six years old, a lawyer who consulted at my workplace convinced me that I needed legal advice from him. I had recently broken up with my boyfriend with whom I co-owned a property. We had plans in place about how to divide the asset fairly and I had no concerns. But this man, let's call him 'Bozo', insisted that I needed to be careful and that I should meet him after work to discuss how to protect myself from being taken advantage of by my ex-boyfriend.

Assuming that Bozo had more knowledge about legal matters than I did, I agreed. I think I even expressed some gratitude for his concern and willingness to make sure I would be okay. All the while I questioned whether I needed Bozo's help because I actually still had good relationship with my ex and trusted him. But self-doubt had me thinking, 'What if Bozo's right? What if I'm not considering some important aspect of my situation?'

Within 20 minutes of arriving at the restaurant we'd agreed on, Bozo was hitting on me. I was still heartbroken because of the split from my boyfriend and had no interest in that kind of attention from anyone, let alone a married man almost twice my age to whom I was not at all attracted. Rather than giving him a flat-out 'no' because I feared being disrespectful or offending him, I curiously questioned him using a deliberately surprised tone, "Don't you have a wife and child at home?" He condescendingly responded, "Marriages are complex," as if I was too naïve to understand such matters.

Had this experience happened to me in more recent years, I'd have left the restaurant, not giving even a second thought to the meal that had already been ordered. But not before looking him square in the eye and saying, "You have no right to disrespect me or misrepresent yourself or your intentions in order to lure me to this unnecessary meeting. You've wasted my time and if you ever do it again, I'm going to call your wife and let her know what kind of scum you are."

I wasn't empowered enough at twenty-six to speak up like that to a man in his position. So I uncomfortably sat through the meal and one glass of wine, while he had at least four wines and got quite drunk. I made small talk and counted the minutes until about 8pm – when it seemed not-too-rude to say, 'Oh, it's getting late, I've got to go'. He insisted on walking me to my car. I only agreed because my car was parked on a busy, well-lit main road. I exhaled with relief when I was finally driving away from Bozo, especially as he tried to grab on to me just before I got into my car. And I did not answer my phone when he called twice at about 1am.

I cringe at how timid I was in that situation and how little I spoke up. I feel some guilt about not speaking up to my employers the next day when I think about how he may have done this to other women too. But I feared his prestigious position and connections within the community would make my experience count for very little. I feared he'd deny the experience and I'd be made to look like a fool in front of my employers. I feared the response I'd get was 'Why did you agree to go out to dinner with him?'

Through older, wiser eyes, and with much more confidence and self-esteem than I had back then, I can see that his behaviour that night was not at all my fault. Not one little bit. I feel angry when I think back to that night. I've considered calling him to say what I wish I'd said that night and even did an Internet search for him. But after searching for five minutes and not finding him, I let it go. Part of me was relieved to have not found him and simply put the matter behind me. But should I ever hear of a woman pressing charges against Bozo, I'll be one of the women coming out of the woodwork to say, "me too". I'll do this without hesitation even though I believe the responses fired back at me will include, "Well, why didn't you complain about it at the time?"

I didn't stand up for myself at the time because I was too indoctrinated by a system designed to keep me quiet, self-doubting and 'in my place'. I was too scared – not to go up against a person, but to go up against a system at a time when I didn't even have the knowledge, understanding or wherewithal to say the words "a system". I lived within the system. I was not aware of it or its power over me.

Now, as much as I resent how Bozo behaved, I'm more resentful of a culture that enables these kinds of encounters, or much worse, to happened hundreds of times a day. Or validates comments such as 'What was she wearing?' or 'Boys will be boys'. Or labels a man as a 'strong leader' but a woman as 'bossy' for the same behaviour. Or in any way attempts to disempower women simply because they're women, or expects men to fit into a rigid definition of masculinity. I'm simply not buying into that narrative anymore.

It can be challenging to go against the system narrative. But the fact remains, systems can and do change – quicker if we push for it.

OUTDATED RULES

Dear Sister, when you were a child, your mind created a whole set of rules about how to survive this life – to experience happiness and avoid pain.

Sometimes you tested the rules. Maybe you took something you weren't supposed to. Maybe you had a tantrum. Maybe you negotiated with parents to get something you wanted. Regardless of whether you succeeded, you always found further reinforcement about where the boundaries are and who's in charge.

Those rules were perfect rules for the time you created them. They were perfect for when you were small and almost all the people around you were bigger than you; sometimes a lot bigger. Perfect for when you were dependent on grown-ups for your survival. Perfect for when your most important needs, like food, water, clothes and sleep, were provided by someone else.

To varying degrees, those childhood rules always stay with you. If you haven't taken the time to work on yourself and update your rules so they are more relevant to your current environment, you will continue to live by those old rules. You might find yourself in your twenties or thirties or even older, seeking approval from others as though your life depends on it.

I regularly meet women who have seemingly forgotten they have a job, drive a car and raised children. They have travelled, been promoted or run businesses, and are educated. And yet, each of these women seems to have forgotten her survival is not dependent on anyone but herself.

Sister, watch out you don't get so forgetful. You may work for accolades. And there's nothing inherently wrong with enjoying praise or compliments. But don't for a second think you need *approval from others to be okay.*

As a grown woman, a rule like 'I need approval from others' is long outdated.

REALISING

POWER

Alice Walker, author of *The Color Purple*, said, "The most common way people give up their power is by believing they don't have any."

That's it. People simply choose to align themselves with limiting beliefs rather than identifying with the power they have.

Why, if we can choose to believe anything we want, would we choose to believe anything other than 'I am powerful'?

No one is going to hand the status of 'powerful' to us. Instead, the prevailing culture can leave us feeling like we have no right to even take up space, let alone stand in our power.

But we don't need permission. On the contrary, if someone attempts to make us feel small or unworthy, it is our responsibility not to believe them.

We mustn't let our own psyches be the reason for our disempowerment. Instead, we need to grab onto the belief in our own power, and protect it vigilantly.

YOU ARE THE PLACEBO

Dear Sister, you are the placebo.

You already have all the power you need, but first you need to believe it.

Take a dose of you every day, more if needed. Recall all the times you failed but got back up again. Swallow that pill. Remember how, in spite of being told you'd fail, you succeeded. Swallow that one too.

Think about every time you've mended your broken heart. And every loss you've suffered and survived.

You sometimes felt like you wouldn't survive pain like that. You thought you'd never be happy again. Or wouldn't recover from the loss.

But all evidence to the contrary.

So whatever you may be going through now, or what challenges you encounter in the future, look back and remember.

Then look forward and know.

CONFUITION

If I ask a woman how many times she has ignored, doubted or disregarded her intuition, it's a rhetorical question. I know it happens. A lot. I've worked with so many women and I've seen it over and over.

We doubt intuition far more than we should. If we check in with intuition right now, she'll confirm this.

So let's be clear, lack of intuition is not the problem. We already have as much intuition as we are ever going to need, even if we haven't acknowledged it yet. Having the courage to back it up is the issue – to follow through on what we already know we should do.

When it comes to creating the outcomes we want, intuition is wonderful, but it's not enough. Intuition is passive. It's about listening. It's very important, but it doesn't create anything on its own. We need to collaborate with inner wisdom, not just sit there taking notes.

We need to be in cahoots with intuition, conspiring and taking action towards our most authentically lived, big love, no regrets life. There is no logical reason to be sitting back waiting for a sign. We need to pick up the brush and paint that thing ourselves.

We need to strut through life as if we own it. Because we do. This life is our privilege and what we make of it is our responsibility. Nobody is coming to save us (and if they are, they are not serving our empowerment).

This critical combination of confidence and intuition is what I call *confuition*.

Confuition is active. It's intuition in action. It's inner wisdom moving you head on, with heart pounding, towards the light. Sometimes, the light is almost blinding, like driving into the setting sun. It can feel unsafe, but we can adjust the speed and the sun visor and continue moving forward. We sense the call of our destination and we keep going.

DANCE ON THE ASHES

MAKE YOUR MOVE

Dear Sister, turning your most exciting vision for your life into reality requires courageous action.

Are you ready? Don't worry if you're not. It's a process. You can start by simply adopting a word that combines your intuition with a whole lot of action: Confuition.

It might feel strange at first. It did for me and sometimes I got confused looks from others. I didn't let that deter me however, because I know how powerful words can be.

Words send a powerful message to yourself about how to behave. Simply changing a word can change how you feel and experience life. A word change can take you from keeping yourself small to standing up straighter, prouder and ready to claim your space in the world.

Your time is now. Your space is here.

Choose your words. Stake your claim. Make your move.

[The story of] your life depends on it.

IT'S NOT OKAY TO LET PEOPLE DOWN, OR IS IT?

Renee, a coaching client, was feeling really guilty about having let someone down. In the previous week, she made a choice between two job roles. She made her decision after much deliberation, including, exploring how to do the right thing by everyone involved, more deliberation (and some worry), weighing up pros and cons, and exploring worst case scenarios.

Renee had done all her due diligence. Yet, after she had informed all the relevant people about her decision, she spiralled into guilt about letting down the person whose job offer she'd declined. I listened to her describe how much she liked the woman who'd offered her the job, how grateful she was to have had the offer, and how guilty she felt about saying no.

After gaining clarity about Renee's situation, I politely interrupted and asked:

Where is the rule that says, 'It's not okay to let people down?'

This confounded Renee. It was immediately obvious that she'd never seriously questioned this rule before. Nor had she considered the possibility that it might actually be okay to let someone down.

As Renee pondered this new concept, it was clear that a whole world of possibilities was opening up for her. Her realm of possibility was expanding in real-time as she contemplated a reality in which she could be free of being responsible for other people's happiness.

As we continued to explore this new world, we clarified three key things:

First, letting people down is not the goal. Of course it's not. We still care about people and their feelings. We still aim to create a win/win wherever we can. If we need to let people down, we aim to do that respectfully and with empathy. If after all that, another person feels let down, we surrender to that part of the process. We give that person responsibility for their own feelings, just as we can take responsibility for our own feelings when we feel that someone has let us down.

Second, it's not logical to *assume* the other person will feel hurt. It's possible Renee was thinking too highly of herself, believing that declining the job offer would hurt or offend the person who had offered it to her. While the other person likely hoped Renee would say yes, they may not have been upset by Renee's decision. They may already have a Plan B they are happy to implement (e.g. they may have a second person in mind for the job).

Third, if we know for a fact the other person feels disappointed or let down (either because it's obvious or they told us), it does not mean they will continue to feel that way. Nor does it mean the event shouldn't have happened. We all have at least one story about something that happened that was challenging or 'bad'. But then, when we recall the incident months or years down the track, we're glad it happened (e.g. Now that I'm married to the love of my life, I'm glad my ex-boyfriend broke my heart).

It may not even take long for someone to adopt a new, more optimistic perspective. The most optimistic people, even in the middle of challenging times, tend to say things like, 'This is not what I wanted and I'm not sure what I'm going to do about it, but I'm confident things will somehow work out for the best'.

This was my response back when I was made redundant from a job. The two managers responsible for giving me the 'bad' news looked very concerned and sympathetic for me. I did appreciate their concern and I could see their decision wasn't personal, and I thought to myself, '*Somehow this is for the best. There were things about this role I didn't enjoy but I was too afraid to leave the security of my job. I don't really know how it's going to work out, and I do feel scared, but part of me is glad they are forcing me outside of my comfort zone. I'm going to trust that I can handle whatever happens next and do my best to turn my predicament into an opportunity.*'

And I did. It was stressful at times and there were many moments of self-doubt, but that redundancy helped me to create a business that I love. So while it's nice to know they cared about my welfare, in reality, if either of those managers lost sleep before giving the redundancy news, or if they spent any time feeling bad or guilty about it, it would have been a waste of their time.

THE ONLY TWO PEOPLE YOU NEED TO IMPRESS

Dear Sister, there's really only two people you need to impress. If these people aren't happy, then life will never feel quite right. When they are happy, everything else seems manageable.

First, your eight-year-old self. She believes in magic and the imaginary. She'll believe almost any dream or fantasy that someone shares with her. She regularly makes decisions based on promises and fairy tales, and she'll run towards them with little care for potential dangers. This is what makes her so delightful – her innocence and absolute faith in dreams and magic.

On the flipside, she is also a bit naïve and needy. When dreams are shattered or magic turns out to be trickery or façade, she crumbles. Like most children, she innocently believes she is like the sun and the world revolves around her. She cannot be reasoned with. She just needs love and understanding.

It's up to you to let her know everything is going to be okay. When you reassure her you'll protect and provide for her always, she'll calm down. It's up to you to be everything for her you ever needed when you were eight years old.

The other person you need to impress is your eighty-year-old self. When you turn your attention to her, she won't waste any time bringing wisdom and incontrovertible truth to the present moment. She is always poised to remind you about all the things you'll regret in the future if you don't take action now.

Your eighty-year-old self can't be bothered with superficial details and she has little patience when you want to indulge in insecurities. If you're in a relationship but crying a lot, she might say something like, "Are you dating a man or an onion? Wake up, girl, you have far too much love to *give and good work to do in this world to waste time on a man who doesn't deserve you." And she will be right. She stopped caring about what others think and she wants you to do the same.*

Focusing on keeping your eighty year old self happy is a sure way to live a life of integrity. If you make a promise to yourself or someone else, she expects you to keep it. She will hold you accountable to living the life you dream about while you still have the time.

THE DEATH CLOCK

I just spent a minute, rather mesmerised, looking at the World Death Clock. I was researching this book and curious about how many people die every day. Next thing I know, I am staring at the clock of death on the Internet. It sounds morbid, but creating the confronting feeling of morbidity was the point – though it worked a little too well for my liking. The clock just keeps ticking over, non-stop, and each number on the clock represents another person who has just died. During that minute, approximately 106 people died – 1.8 people per second.

Some people go to bed, like every other night, and then simply never wake up again. What proof do I have that I will wake up tomorrow? While the answer to this question makes me uncomfortable, I also feel the power in the question. Death reminds us to live with purpose and intention.

I once read that death *teaches* us how to live. I don't agree. Mostly, we already know what we need to do. But we don't do what we know we should do because we're too scared to act on our intuition. We're worried about failing, what others will think and we don't value ourselves enough. Plus, we usually think we have more time. Death reminds us we might not have as much time as we think. It *reminds* us that we need to get out there and pursue the life we want while we still can.

Perhaps I should wake up to the death clock every day. If I could learn to do that without invoking a state of anxiety, then it might serve to make me more present to every moment. It might remind me to savour each moment and be grateful for it. It might also empower me to do all the things I know I'd do if I knew it were my last day.

The thing is, I decided the most important thing for me to do today (and every day for the next couple of months) was write. So that's how I chose to spend today. Even though it takes discipline to actually sit down and write, my soul will keep calling me to write it until it's done. And even though I usually find writing hard, having written makes me happy. So today I wrote.

But if I knew today was my last day, I probably wouldn't continue writing a book that, if I die, won't be finished and will likely never be read, let alone published. I'd probably choose to spend the day with people who are important to me, or go to places that bring me joy one last time.

Upon reflection, the answer is not to live every day as if it's my last. I need to assume I will have more days to create, learn, grow, love and experience joy. Without that assumption, there is a risk that I might not even begin. But I also need to ensure that when I get to my last day, I arrive there without regrets.

The answer is courage. If I live every day with the courage to listen to my intuition and act on it, no matter the outcome or when my last day is, I will have no regrets.

KYLIE ZEAL

DO WHAT IS TRUE FOR YOU

Dear Sister, when your time is done, life will continue.

The birds will still fly. The tides will still rise. And fall. And rise. And continue always to follow the moon.

Some memory of you will remain, but eventually that too shall fade. Along with it, all expectations that were ever placed upon you will be gone.

So let not outside expectation weigh heavy on you now.

Do what is true for you.

Now is your time to be happy.

DANCE ON THE ASHES

SOMETHING TO LOSE

I feel afraid in a way I hadn't expected.

I always wanted a life with a lot of freedom in it and I've worked smart (and sometimes hard) to create it. It took a lot of discipline and courage. I had to (and still do often) practice delayed gratification. I did a lot of self-development to gain clarity about what I want and how stop self-sabotaging my own progress. And I ventured through the pain of letting go of things, people and habits that didn't align with my values.

Though I'm still building my vision, I have in many ways created the freedom I craved. It's amazing and I feel... afraid.

I also feel empowered, happy and free. But let's talk about this feeling of fear. Because I thought I'd *only* feel empowered, happy and free. I thought creating my life of freedom would give me immunity from being afraid. But no. It's more like I've created this amazing life, and now I have something to lose.

When I noted the fear of 'something to lose' I knew I needed to check myself. I discussed what I was experiencing with a good friend and she was very helpful because I often imagined she didn't have fears like mine. She had a waiting list for her business services much longer than mine, so surely she was free from fear? She empathised and said, "It's relative. If my waiting list is three months, then I start thinking I'll feel more secure when it's four months, and so on. And if the waiting list drops to less than three months, I need to watch out fear doesn't send me into a downward spiral. I need to consciously tell myself regularly that it's going to be okay and act accordingly."

Hearing my friend say this, I was frustrated and freed. I was frustrated it would always be my responsibility to ensure fear doesn't get the better of me. But I was also freed by knowing the security and happiness I longed for could be mine, in any moment, regardless of what is going on outside me. I still mitigate against risks in practical ways. But otherwise, I can consciously choose to place my attention on gratitude for what I already have and optimism for the future.

It takes a lot of faith. And faith requires courage. So I take a breath, relax and find my courage and faith because I know this for sure:

Giving time to worrying about losing something does not mean I have insurance against losing it.

If that thing or person is suddenly taken from my life, then I will look back at all the time I'd spent in worry and fear of loss and wish I'd been more present instead. I'd wish I had fully enjoyed the moment while I still had the chance.

WORRY IS NOT INSURANCE

Dear Sister, worry robs you of joy in the present moment.

It is not insurance; it will not protect you against future pain. At best, worry can be a tool. It may provide warnings that prompt you to take action. But without thoughtful action, worry is just worry.

Certainty, on the other hand, is just as much a product of your imagination as worry. How different the outcomes, though?

When you tell yourself stories that incite worry, what does that do for the creation of your life? How energetically do you move forward when worry is your driver? How creative are you? How loving? How happy?

What about your stories that create feelings of certainty? Think about them now and notice how you breathe easier. Notice the urge to move forward when you tell yourself, "I will achieve my vision. At *a minimum, I am sure I can handle the outcome, whatever it turns out to be."*

Stories about certainty are no more a guarantee than stories about worry are insurance. And there is little difference in the amount of energy it takes for your mind to conjure them. But with such a different impact on how you feel and behave, in which story would you like to plant the seeds of your future.

The soil of certainty is fertile and growth inducing. It's the mulch of inspiration. And where the seeds of innovation are cracked open; their essence bursting out, reaching for the sun.

The dirt of worry is dry and cracked. Aside from the weeds, it's where plants and dreams eventually die.

ANXIETMENT

Lately I've been feeling a lot of anxietment.

I love this word – anxietment. I wasn't able to find it in any of the standard dictionaries, and for a while I thought I'd invented it. But then a friend found it for me in an online dictionary.

Anxietment is the perfect word to capture the feeling of being both anxious and excited, which is a common experience for anyone stretching themselves and pursing their dreams. It's the place my coaching clients have usually arrived at before the end of our first coaching session – excited to be one significant step closer to their dreams and anxious about being outside of their comfort zone.

I wrote an article about five years ago called, 'It's a fine line between scared and excited.' So this is not an entirely new concept to me. In my article, I described a conversation I had with a client, Janelle. She had been talking about an opportunity that was 'scary' and made her nervous. I agreed the situation was scary for her. But given it was also an amazing opportunity, I asked her, "Is it scary or is it exciting?" She immediately responded, "Both."

The problem was, Janelle was giving her emotional state just one label: 'scared'. A lot of people do this, and we can hardly blame them, since the experiences of 'scared' and 'excited' are very similar. Both create tension in the body as possible futures are imagined.

We need to acknowledge anxiety when it's present. Fear can be a wise advisor and can teach us many things about ourselves. But fear also needs to be kept in check so it doesn't prevent us from taking action.

We also need to acknowledge excitement when it is present. This is very important. Excitement is a way of acknowledging all the ways we are creating, evolving and succeeding. And it's fuel that keeps us going.

WORDS ARE LIKE KEYS

Dear Sister, watch your words.

Like a key unlocking a door, there are words that unlock a world of possibilities.

And, like a key, a word can lock you out. It can paralyse you, keeping you exactly where you are, never moving forward.

Depending on their context, words like 'maybe', 'yes' or 'no' can open new possibilities. In a different context, these same words could lock you in.

Words are powerful enough to unlock an entire relationship. Or destroy it.

Words can end dreams. 'I can't' is often a dream-killer. As is 'I'll fail'.

The point is, words are powerful. Actions follow words. So use them consciously. Use words that open up your world.

RECKONING

LOVE IS

Wise people say, "Love is the answer." Apparently, no matter the question, love is the answer.

Talk about vague! I spend most of my days with the intention of love. But the ways it looks when put into action are many and varied.

Love should be the intention. I know this for sure now. When I choose how to put love into action, however, I take in many variables for consideration. I take in the people involved, their histories and personalities. I consider the time of day and month and whether I've eaten recently, because I know these can affect my mood. I think about the culture and global climate. I consider my own values and happiness requirements. I attempt to factor in unknown elements. And I assess the predicted outcome.

At least these are all the things I take into account on a good day, when I'm living as my best and most authentic, empathetic and courageous self. Not every day is a good day, though. Some days, I feel tired or scared or frustrated and this can cloud my judgement.

But even on a good day, the choice about how to enact love is rarely easy.

On my journey so far, I've learned that the one singular intention for love has many possible expressions…

Love can be steadfast. No matter what happens, it will always be there.

Love walks away. In spite of giving our all and caring deeply, in spite of feeling like a failure, love bows out, defeated.

Love is a long embrace.

Love pushes someone away.

Love is speaking what's in our hearts. It's sharing our truth even when our heart is pounding and we fear love won't be returned.

Love is staying silent. Even when we know the truth. Especially when the truth will be a mighty blow. Love keeps words unspoken.

Love says, "Yes."

Love says, "Hell, no."

Love exercises regularly. It also eats carrots and leafy greens.

Love stretches out on the sofa. It devours ice-cream and indulges in chocolate, especially champagne truffles.

Love is open and easy going.

Love draws clear boundaries.

Love says, "I will walk to the ends of the Earth with you."

Love says, "Leave if you have to. I'm not going anywhere."

Love is the softest, gentlest touch.

Love is rage. It is fierce and can't be fucked with.

Love turns a blind eye. It empathises with transgressions.

Love says, "Not on my watch." It demands justice.

Love is naïve. It's hopeful, optimistic and wears blurry lenses.

Love is wise. It's been around the block more times than it cares to count and it's a realist.

Love rushes in. It's excited, impetuous and madly committed.

Love is infinitely patient. Free from anxiety, full of certainty, it will faithfully wait.

People often try to tell us what love is or what it's supposed to look like. Sometimes, they make our love seem wrong because our choices and actions don't align with their definition of love.

But love is not rigid in its definitions. Only we can know, if we are honest with ourselves, the truth about whether our intentions, words and actions are sourced in love.

Choose with love and love the choices you make. That's all we can really do anyway because we have no guarantee about the outcome or response.

Love knows how to, and will, adjust when necessary. Love is flexible. Love can pause – even if just for a moment – long enough to make a different choice when needed.

LIFE BESET WITH LOVE CHALLENGES

Dear Sister, if it doesn't feel like love, it probably isn't. Except for when it is.

Confused? Yes, well it's the challenge of a lifetime to know when those around you are being loving.

Starting when you were young, you had people who loved you and who, for loving reasons, took away the thing you wanted. Or forced you to clean your room. Or go to sleep. Or eat vegetables. Or practice your instrument. In hindsight, it might look like love, but it often didn't feel like it at the time Either way, all of these kinds of experiences shape the way we give, receive and interpret love.

Some of the greatest pain you can experience in life is through relationships with people who do not really love you though you wish they would. Their behaviour is quite the opposite of love. And yet, you seek to justify on their behalf because their love is what you want. You willingly take the scraps of evidence that they love you, albeit outweighed by a lifetime of misdeeds.

You might have experienced the confusion, pain and guilt of being in relationship with people who love you, but who can't love you in the way you need. It might be they love you the best way they know how, but their love is immature, controlling or unhealthy. Or you might have experienced when someone loves you, and something tells you their love is good for you, but their loves turns you off.

Maybe you have or will meet a person who you love and who loves you. It all seems to fit and it feels like the love has no beginning – like you've somehow always known them. Still, in time, you realise the person you love is flawed (just like you) and dealing with challenges and conflict is part of being in love.

How do you thrive through a life beset with love challenges?

Fill yourself with love. Fill your tank and fill your reserves. There is no higher priority for your life.

When you are filled with love by your own means, it cannot be taken from you or lost. Self-love is your most important foundation for living with courage and loving in healthy ways.

When you are filled with love, you will make the wisest, best-possible decisions about every form of love you encounter.

I CHOSE ME

Sitting in the dark in my car, I suddenly realised how cold it was. I'd never done a coaching session in my car before, but there I was in the middle of winter, sitting on a quiet backstreet, doors locked, and the street lamp to light my notebook.

It was warm in the car when I started the coaching session. I'd driven the car around for ten minutes to warm up the engine and get the heater going. But I hadn't wanted the sound of the car in the background during the session, so I turned off the engine.

As usual, the coaching was transformational. For a moment after I hung up the phone, I felt gratitude and awe at my client's willingness to face her fears and take on challenges. In the next moment, it was cold. I was back in reality. My reality. A reality that, given my present situation, was clearly not sustainable.

I wondered for a moment whether I should go home. Of course I would. Where else was I going to go? But I wasn't actually going *home*, was I? Surely home is a place where there is space for me to do what I need to and be myself. If I needed to go somewhere else to be me, then perhaps my home was somewhere else.

I felt confused and afraid. *What would my life look like if I changed it? But look at me now; I'm sitting in my car in the dark in the middle of winter. This is not what my life is meant to look like.*

I replayed the earlier events of the night. Should I have done something differently? Should I have been more accommodating? I looked at my phone and saw a message received during the coaching session. It read: I've cleared out the study for you. *Too late*, I thought. *Why did it have to be so hard to get the things I needed?*

When I had arrived home earlier that evening, I was tired from doing coaching sessions all day at the office and it was less than an hour before my final coaching session of the day was due to start. I had walked into the study and greeted my partner like usual. Then I reminded him, "I have a coaching session scheduled for tonight. It will only go for an hour. It's on the phone and I just need a room with a closed door and no interruptions, so I can work from either the study or the bedroom. You tell me which room you want and I'll go in the other."

He responded, "I need both." For a moment I was confused and not sure what to say. Is he serious? "It's just for an hour," I explained. He didn't budge. Apparently, caught up in his own need to be travelling for work the next day, he needed to alternate between the bedroom to pack his bag and the study to do work on his computer. I pushed back again but he was clearly not going to budge without a fight.

I felt stuck, frustrated and confused. *Does he not understand that coaching is how I earn income that contributes to paying for our home and lifestyle?* Immediately I realised that even knowing the answer to this question wouldn't create the outcome I needed in the next 45 minutes. So I walked out of the study and began pacing in the kitchen, trying to work out what I could do, clock ticking.

I realised I was in a lose/lose battle. Even if I continued to push back and he eventually relented and gave me permission to have a room to myself in my own home for an hour, I would then be in a mindset that was not conducive to coaching. I just needed space to do my coaching for one hour. I needed to get out of there. So I grabbed my things and yelled, "I'm going for a drive" as I walked out the door.

I have never again done a coaching session from my car. It was not long after that night that I left the home we shared, and, ultimately, the relationship. Not simply because of this one incident, but because the general theme of our relationship was that I regularly had to give up my needs for him and rarely felt appreciated for doing so. And the ludicrous reality of having to sit in the dark and cold in my car in order to do my job triggered the final reckoning.

I realised, if I stay with this man, I'll never finish my book. If I stay, I am sending the wrong message to the young women in my life I know look up to me. If I stay, I am not demonstrating the courage I expect from my clients. If I stay, I will continue to be treated with much less appreciation, respect and integrity than I am worth.

So, I chose me, even though it was hard and venturing into the unknown is always scary. I chose to let go, even though I knew I would miss him. I chose to leave, even though, if I could, I wouldn't change the past.

I chose me and now, with the benefit of hindsight, it was the right decision. Funny that; every single time I have ever made a choice grounded in self-worth and self-belief, it was the right decision.

YOUR HAPPINESS IS YOUR RESPONSIBILITY

Dear Sister, if I asked you to name all the things you love, how long would it be before you named yourself?

If I asked you to give to yourself, how well could you do that without guilt?

If your life is filled with people who recognise all you give and who give to you in return (whether it be through actions or other evidence of appreciation), you have wisely surrounded yourself with co-conspirators of your flourishing.

But if even one person in your world takes for granted all that you give, it is your responsibility to balance the scales. It's up to you, whenever you're feeling drained, to draw a line in the sand and say, "That's enough for one day."

It seems to go against the nature of giving, but it's quite the opposite. Logic dictates that you cannot give what you do not have. You need to tend to your own needs and growth. You need to rejuvenate and replenish your energy.

Your happiness is your responsibility. It is also your right. So cultivate your gifts. Logic dictates that you cannot harvest what you did not plant, sow and nurture. Invest in activities that make your soul come alive.

Give yourself permission. Ask for help when needed. Forgive yourself when you mess up. Draw the line in the sand when your intuition says it's time. Follow your calling, even when it's scary. And let go of external expectations that conflict with your soul.

Rest assured you will not make everyone happy. But even if you could, it would still begin with first allocating energy to yourself and cultivating your own happiness.

DANCE ON THE ASHES

WHAT'S THE WORST THAT COULD HAPPEN?

My friend Anna is one of the great loves of my life. She married a man who makes her very happy, so I love him too. Through regular conversations with Anna, I understand him to be highly intelligent, adventurous, loving, courageous enough to be vulnerable, self-aware, respectful, hard-working and attractive.

Perhaps, then, you can imagine my surprise when, on a rare daytrip to the countryside (rare because we reside in different countries), just the two of us, she disclosed the unhappy thoughts and feelings she had been harbouring about her marriage.

Clearly, there were some changes going on in their marriage. She was changing, maybe he was too, or, what's more than likely true in any relationship of more than ten years, they both were. And changes often freak people out, especially when things have been good for so long.

Anna didn't want to push expectations on to her husband. She was fully aware of all the great things about him and she felt some guilt at expecting him to change simply because she was making changes. She could also see how her expectations and attitudes were likely contributing to the conflicts they were experiencing.

At the same time, Anna's values and the changes she sought were important to her and she didn't feel willing to let them go. So she began fearing they might not be able to stay together. This thought scared her so much, she hadn't been willing to express it out loud.

Fear is the thing that really messes with our minds and ability to think logically. Experiencing fear is like putting on a pair of prescription glasses that were not made for you. They really blur the way you see the world.

It seemed my dear friend had the fear glasses on. As the outsider who knew her well, this seemed crazy. I knew her to be incredibly resourceful, successful and capable of overcoming any challenge. But that's easier to see when we aren't the ones in the middle of it. Given my vantage point, I decided to ask some questions that might change her perspective, much the same as she does for me when I'm in the middle of an issue and can't see a way out.

Me: Would you like another way of looking at this?

Anna: Yes.

Me: Okay, let's do an exercise that always works for me and my clients. It's a game, and if you're going to play, you need to trust me and play fully. Okay?

Anna: Yes.

Me: Thinking about this situation, tell me, what's the worst that could happen?

Anna: This situation with my husband doesn't get better; it gets worse.

Me: And what would that mean? What's the worst that could happen?

Anna: We break up.

Anna's discomfort with saying the words out loud was palpable. But being uncomfortable is okay. This is the place we need to take ourselves when we are scared. If we want to get past the fear, we need to walk straight up to it, look it in the eye, and keep going. Freedom is on the other side of fear.

Me: Okay, is that the worst, Anna? The two of you breaking up is the worst that could happen?

Anna: Well, it's that we would break up and then I'd be alone. We wouldn't have any more good times together. I'd miss him. I'd be devastated and heartbroken.

Me: Okay, stay with me. You're doing great; keep trusting me. Now, let's imagine the worst has just happened. Even though you know you'll miss him and you're heartbroken, you're getting a divorce. You feel devastated about the loss of a relationship that meant the world to you and all the good times you're no longer going to have in the future. Take yourself to that place, Anna. Imagine that is your current reality. Can you do that?

Anna: Yes.

Me (checking in): How are you feeling right now?

Anna: Uncomfortable. My heart is pounding.

Me: Okay, stay with me. Breath. And when you're ready, tell me, now that the worst has happened, what you are going to do next? What are the plans you are going to put in place? How are you going to live your life given the new circumstances?

Anna: Wow. I don't know.

Me: That's normal. Fear gets in the way of making plans. Keep going.

Anna: I would definitely make plans. I'd make plans for my heart, my health and my soul. I'd work with a coach or a psychologist to help me grow through the transition. I would spend time with friends. I'd keep building my business. Wow, I could really build my business! I'd probably do some travelling. I'd write a book. I'd basically just keep moving and creating all the things in my life that bring me joy.

Me: Would you be okay?

Anna: [laughing uncomfortably] I think I'd be better than okay. I'd probably thrive. It is bad that I think I'd thrive without my husband?

Me: No, it's not bad at all. It's actually great that you now realise you're in a win/win situation. You don't want to break up with your husband. I don't want you to break up with your husband. So, if the two of you can flow with the transition and grow together, ultimately becoming stronger, that's a win! And if it turns out that the relationship has to end, that will be a win too because you already know that if the worst were to happen, you would be sad and heartbroken and eventually you would thrive. Life can always be a win/win situation. And from the perspective of 'life is a win/win', you can have much less fear around the challenges you and your husband are currently experiencing. This is powerful because fear tends to make the situation worse and, ironically, more likely to create the thing you fear.

Anna: This is amazing. I was attempting to control what he was doing because I feared what might happen in the future. I was making up all kinds of stories about what was going on. I was imagining the worst that could happen but I was just staying in that place of fear instead of having trust in myself and him. Now, I can just let him be. He'll work out whatever he needs to work out. I can do the same for me. Of course we will continue to communicate, but we can also give each other space. This way of viewing the situation creates much more room for being loving.

Two years on, Anna and her husband are happier than ever. Most of what we fear never comes to pass. If it does, we can handle it. If we take the time to think about how resourceful we are, especially when we really need to be, we have to admit we have what it takes to handle whatever comes our way.

When we're prepared to use our imagination to work all the way through 'the worst that could happen', we find that we would be able to manage should the unlikely circumstance ever actually happen. It wouldn't be easy, but we would find the strength, procure the resources and make the best of the life we've been given. It is within our control to not only survive challenging times, but thrive in spite of them.

ANSWER THE SCARY QUESTIONS

Dear Sister, life becomes easier when you're willing to answer *hard questions.*

We regularly ask ourselves hard questions like, "What if I fail? What if they reject me? What if I make a mistake? What will they say about me? What if there is something wrong with me?"

But then we don't answer the question; not really. Too often we only take our minds as far as, "Everything will turn to crap" *or* "My life will be over" *or* "I couldn't handle it". *These are not answers. These are the flippant remarks of a mind that is being fearful, tired or lazy.*

These vague responses are known as 'catastrophising' and they prompt us to build a wall within our minds. We then attempt to put those scary questions and their catastrophic answers on the other side of the wall, believing that if we don't think about it, then we are protected from it. It doesn't work though, does it? To some extent, we are always aware of the ever-present danger on the other side of the imaginary wall and we use it as our excuse to not take action.

Sister, empowered living begins with empowered thinking. So, if you ask yourself one of the hard questions, believe in yourself enough to follow that thought all the way to a logical conclusion. Reckon with yourself and acknowledge all the ways you can handle life's inevitable challenges.

What if you fail?

Good question. Yes, what if? What exactly will you do if your plan fails? If you fail? If you let someone down? If someone you love dies? If you and your partner break-up? If you lose your money?

It won't be the end. Even if it feels like the end of your world. It won't be. It will be the beginning of a new stage in your life for which the ending is yet to be written.

There are very, very, very few negative situations that can't be mended, overcome or even reversed. Death would be one of them. If you're taking a risk that includes a realistic possibility that you could end up dead, you really need to take the time to consider alternatives.

For all other outcomes you fear however, if they should ever come to pass, there will be a solution. It may not be easy and *there will be a way forward. It may be tough, but you are tougher.*

So don't just park scary questions into the recesses of your mind and seek distractions from them. Write those stories all the way to the end. Include all the details; all the scary, joyful, horrible, bittersweet, heartbreaking, lovely details that may ensue. It may feel scary, or exciting, or both. Either way, you are innovative, brave and empowered when you choose to be, and you have all the answers you need.

NO MONEY FOR THE RENT

This is not entirely comfortable to share but I think it's important. It all started with a call to my Dad to wish him happy birthday. We ended up getting into a debate because he made a comment about something, in his opinion, I should have done differently a decade ago.

The comment he made (that I should have bought another investment property ten years ago), as far as general statements go, was probably good advice. But once my Dad had made the comment, there were instantly three issues present in the dialogue:

1. The statement lacked consideration of variables that were unique to me.
2. He was pointing out something that had happened ten years ago (i.e. I can't change what happened yesterday, let alone what happened ten years ago!)
3. His comment triggered insecurities I already have around finances, investments and money.

One of the things I love about my Dad is that he stays in the conversation. That might sound like an easy thing to do, but it's not easy once a conversation become heated and your daughter is feeling wrongly judged for past decisions.

Many people shut down, or run away, or get angry and defensive when conversations with people they care about get heated. Not my Dad. He stays in the conversation, he rarely gets defensive and he listens. I mean, he *really* listens.

His listening became the gift he gave me on his birthday. As I thought back to ten years ago, to justify decisions I had made at that time in my life, I remembered things I don't think about much these days. And they were empowering reminders.

You see, twelve years ago, I made the decision to go back to university to study Psychology. I remembered how much courage I had to find in order to leave full time employment and become a student again. I also remembered how much faith I had to find in myself in order to enrol in my coaching accreditation during the same period. That was a 12 month course I did alongside my degree and I took out a payment plan for the $9,000 expense (in addition to the financial loan I was accumulating for university fees). Not to mention all the evenings and weekends invested in completing assignments rather than socialising with friends.

I also remembered how, about ten years ago, my part-time job that supported me while I studied was made redundant. The uncertainty that created was really freakin' scary. But I placed faith in myself that I could make it work... somehow... and I decided, rather than look for another job, I would start my own coaching business.

Anyone who has ever started their own business will tell you it takes time to create momentum. My business was no different. So you see, instead of being in a position to buy another investment property ten years ago, I was paying my rent with my credit card.

That was hard for me and it was out of character. It was one of the only periods in my life that I wasn't paying off my entire credit card balance at the end of each month. But there I was, using my credit card to make sure the rent was paid.

As I recounted all this to my Dad, I said, "I may not have invested in another property ten years ago, but I made investments. I invested in me, and I believe that investment will pay off far more than a property ever will."

"We are still yet to see exactly how the investments in myself will pay off financially, but I don't even care much about that because I already feel they have paid off by protecting me against the regret of staying in a career I didn't enjoy. Each day in that job, it felt like my soul was dying."

"I don't feel like that anymore. Maybe it won't be possible for me to retire in my fifties because of decisions I made in the past, but I now do a job that I don't feel like I need to retire from. Why would I ever want to retire from doing what I love?"

I felt the truth of every word I had spoken.

I felt myself exhale as I had a moment of realisation – *I am courageous. I paid my dues and earned this life I love. I still have a way to go to achieve my ever expanding vision but I'm already successful.* Thank you Father for reminding me that we can't measure ourselves against 'general advice' that may be good for the masses, and for always listening.

ADVICE CONVERTER

Dear Sister, every decision you have made, and will make, is based on variables unique to you.

No-one has walked every step you trod. Or seen every moment through your eyes. Or heard the whispers of your soul.

That won't stop friends and strangers from giving you advice along the journey. Sometimes it's exactly what you need to hear. And some opinions come with the best of intentions. Still, you need to filter all information through your internal converter — to make sure it's relevant to you. It's like exchanging a foreign currency. It had value where it came from but it might need to be converted before you can utilise its value in your life.

When you've completed the conversion, is the wisdom still useful to you? Does it still hold value? Will the choices you make about what to pursue outweigh what you will inevitably give up?

There is always a giving up. For anything you choose to pursue, there is a price to be paid. An opportunity-cost. Time spent.

One stage of maturity involves accepting all those things you will never do, or have, in exchange for the things you choose. And the person who pays the cost is you.

So while the good opinions of others might hold value, or may have been delivered by someone you hold in high esteem with pure intentions, any advice received on your journey to happiness must flow through your soul's converter.

THE EVERYDAY GOOD STUFF

One morning, half way between my apartment door and the elevator, I found a young man sitting in the hall, surrounded by balloons.

I caught his attention as he was blowing up one of the balloons. With his finger across his smiling lips, looking half embarrassed and half hopeful, I immediately understood his polite request to refrain from making too much noise. With his free hand, he moved a few balloons, creating a path for me to access the elevator, and he whispered something about a birthday.

Though I didn't hear exactly what he said, I understood the intention, the action and the love. And as I witnessed it unfolding, I was mentally transported back to the apartment in a little town outside of Birmingham, England, that I shared with my boyfriend at the time when we were both in our early twenties.

The apartment was above a shop and it had a whole lot of character, which is a nice way of saying it was old and the washing machine was situated in the middle of one of the bedrooms. It was perfect and such a fun time in my life. I was in love and one of the ways I expressed it was by setting an alarm clock for 2am under my pillow (so only I'd hear it) on my boyfriend's birthday. I snuck out of bed and crept down to the 'washing room' at the other end of our apartment. Then I spent the next hour or so blowing up balloons with a little plastic pump. Thank goodness for that little plastic pump, otherwise I'm sure I'd never have got through all the balloons by sunrise.

I slowly and quietly moved all the balloons to our bedroom, covering the entire floor, and crept back into bed for some more sleep. In the morning, I opened my eyes to my boyfriend's grinning face only inches from mine. I'll never forget that look or the joy, even now, almost two decades later.

As I watched this young man with the balloons in the hall of my apartment building, I was reminded once again, *this is the everyday good stuff.*

In a world that it not always good and in which terrible things happen, there is good. In a world that would have us believe there is something missing, that we need to compensate for all of the ways we are flawed, that we need to be afraid, there is good.

It may not be the polished and rehearsed kind of 'good' that is portrayed in movies and advertising. It's the messy, fumble our words, sometimes misunderstood but well intentioned, kind of 'good' that is real. And it's everywhere – if we look for it.

It's the man who yells for the tram driver to wait because I've almost missed my opportunity to disembark at my stop. It's dance parties in the living room with my five-year-old step-daughter while Keith Urban sings 'Somebody Like You' loudly on the stereo. It's speaking to my dear friend overseas as soon as I wake up every Tuesday. Or my father calling me every Wednesday. It's the friend who looks at me like her heart is breaking when she knows my heart is breaking. Or the genuine joy she feels when my life is going well. This is the everyday good stuff.

It's every bedtime story and good night hug. It's the way my partner looks at me like I'm astonishingly beautiful; even after 23 years of knowing me; even when I'm sure I look terrible. It's every time you laugh till you cry, especially in the company of friends. It's every bunch of flowers ever given with love. It's all the people who volunteer their time to help even though they're busy. It's every time someone does something kind and decent simply because they know it's the kind and decent thing to do. This is the everyday good stuff.

I'd like to see the everyday good stuff presented in daily news broadcasts. But we rarely see such things because they aren't 'news'. They are not dramatic or extraordinary. They are ordinary. They are more common than we realise because media would have us believe that evil and tragedy outweigh good; because the media preys on our susceptibility to scaremongering and because money flows where attention goes. As a journalist friend said to me, "The media thrives on conflict. Good news stories are nice, but they don't rate." So, while the media is part of the problem by focusing so much on the negative, we are also the problem because we allow our attention to be drawn to it.

Have no doubt, evil and hatred exist. But to what extent? Compared to what? This is the reckoning that needs to take place at the end of every day.

We mustn't ignore the hateful stuff. On the contrary, we need to stop it. But we also need to ensure it doesn't overwhelm us and blind us to all that is good. Being overwhelmed can lead to anger or apathy. Anger can be powerful and useful if it's based in love and disciplined. But too often anger is undisciplined and further perpetuates hate and misunderstandings. Apathy often means no action, which can be all that evil needs to continue.

When we remember love, like that which exists in the everyday good stuff, it reminds us that we have something worth taking a stand for. It creates perspective and effective thinking. It fuels the courage and confidence we need to take action and create more of the everyday good stuff.

FOCUS

Dear Sister, everything falls into place when you focus on what you have instead of what's missing.

Not to say, you simply ignore those things in life that aren't working. Rather, you take what 'isn't working' and place it within the context of what is.

Focusing on what you have and what's working will create three powerful insights for dealing with challenges: perspective, possibility and patience.

Perspective – All problems are a matter of perspective. From certain angles, problems are gifts. At a minimum, they are always an opportunity to learn, grow and evolve.

Possibility – There is always another way. Fear puts your attention on problems. Gratitude reveals opportunity.

Patience – When you see the positives in what you have now, you won't be in such a *hurry to always get to the next place. Your calm will in turn help you create your nest stage more effectively.*

There is more you want from life, and that's okay. But everything you most need, you already have within you.

NO MORE BS

There were times I bullshitted my therapist. Of all the people I shouldn't have needed to bullshit, surely she should have been the most obvious. I paid her to listen to all my stuff and keep it a secret. Non-judgement and empathy is part of her job. And the purpose of therapy, ultimately, is to move beyond one's own stuff, especially the stuff preventing forward movement, success and happiness. But I couldn't move beyond all the stifling bullshit if I wasn't willing to admit that it was there.

I didn't really mean to deceive my therapist. I just didn't know how to do life differently from the way I'd been doing it up until that point. No, what I knew how to do was show up to the session and give my therapist the play-by-play account of the latest episode in the drama that was my life.

My life drama included a series of episodes revolving around my pseudo-relationship with a narcissistic, commitment-phobic man. He often made little gestures of affection and was great with random text messages. I was determined to have my therapist sold on the idea that those gestures made up for the ninety-five percent of the time that he was emotionally and physically unavailable.

My therapist, bless her, listened and consoled throughout all of it. Most of the time, she empathetically went along with my stories, probably because my stories were quite convincing. Then, one day, I said something that must have tipped her off. I don't even remember what it was. I just remember her telling me in a subtle but fierce tone, "He's a snake."

I don't remember exactly what I said back to her but I remember how I felt. I was caught between wanting to retaliate against the person who was threatening to devalue all evidence that the pseudo-relationship [to which I was attaching my self-identity] was worth something, and needing to accept that she'd called 'bullshit' on me and could be right.

If I could transport my current self back in time, that is one of the moments I'd visit. I'd walk into that therapy room and I'd high-five my therapist. I'd then look my younger self in the eye and say, "Buuuuuullshiiiiiiit."

And as my twenty-something self sat there stunned and unsure which side of her internal battle to get on, I'd look at her with genuine love and empathy and I'd say, "Have faith. There are going to be extraordinary people and experiences in your life and, right now, you can't even imagine them. About five years from now, you're going to, finally, get really bored with all this unnecessary drama because you'll realise it doesn't lead anywhere except misery. You'll finally wake up to the truth that your worth depends on nothing but a decision from you, and that will be all you need to create a totally different life."

"About ten years from now, this same guy is going to invite you to a fancy event, and you'll have no interest in attending. He's a wounded little boy in a man's body, and even ten years from now he'll still be attempting to manipulate everyone around him to compensate for all the ways he feels insecure – only you'll no longer have any inclination to play a role in his drama. When you let go of all the fear and your insecurities, it'll free you up to find one of the greatest joys you'll ever experience. Trust me. You don't know this yet, but you're a writer. You will evolve to a level of self-assurance and confidence that, right now, is not even in your realm of possibility. But you'll get there and when you do, you'll start writing."

"So stop with the BS and the drama and have faith. Much better things are on their way to you and it will have very little to do with luck. Rather, you will experience more joy in your life in direct proportion to the level you rise above the drama and see your whole life through a wider lens. When you focus on what you have instead of what's missing. When you begin using your gifts and talents instead of wasting time worrying about what others think."

"You know I'm right. At least you want to believe me, but it's scary. I get that; I've been there. Every time you walk away, even when it's in the name of self-worth, it will feel like an ending. It will have been a period of your life that actually meant something to you, and that you thought would turn out better than it did. You will feel sad for the loss and it will be scary moving into an unknown future."

"But keep moving. Every ending is actually a beginning. The partner, career, friendships and experiences that bring you joy all come into your life when you make space for them by saying no to anything that resembles low self-worth or lack of self-respect."

"It will happen when you take a stand for your life. Trust me, I've seen it. So get ready."

FAITH MUST BE YOUR CONVICTION

Dear Sister, imagine sitting down to chat with your future-self. She's a few decades older than you and, as an orange-red sun sets in the distance, you notice she looks very happy. She smiles at you. She knows you well, of course. She's been where you are and she's lived your mistakes and achievements. So she has much greater depth of retrospect and you're interested to learn her wisdom.

The two of you discuss the most important things in your life and you look to her for guidance. She tells you, "There is nothing I know that you don't already know." She pauses to let that sink in. She knows you doubt your wisdom.

Then she continues: "You already have the most powerful insights you need. The most fundamental laws of life are not a secret and we learned them young. Some of that knowledge is intuitive, and some of it is external and has been around longer than we have. What I do have, that you don't yet, is conviction.

In all the years that I've lived longer than you, I've acquired very little new knowledge. What I've gained through my experiences was evidence. Like most people, I've spent time testing life's laws to prove to myself they are true. And I can tell you, they are."

"You intuitively know you won't ever be completely happy until you are living in alignment with your true self and following the calling of your soul. Until then, you'll feel like something is missing."

"You'll feel most alive when you're willing to risk failure and take a chance on those things that feel important to you. Regardless of whether it works out as you hoped, you will feel empowered, courageous and in love with yourself because you overcame fear and took action. You will feel inner contentment *simply by being on the path you know is right for you, rather than one dictated by others. Because, in this lifetime, the final destination is not the point. The process of taking the journey dictated by your soul will deliver the superior experience."*

"Don't wait for someone else to approve of you. Give the approval to yourself. Give yourself permission to take chances, to risk looking like a fool, and to get over it fast if you do ever look foolish."

"Let go of external opinions. Most people don't really know you and their opinions reflect much more how they experience the world than anything about you. Even though it can seem like other people have life figured out, in truth, they are second-guessing themselves just as much as the rest of us. Second-guessing is often a necessary part of making decisions and progress, but third, fourth and fifth-guessing is too much self-doubt. Just go for it. Being able to error-correct when necessary is much better for

progress and happiness than attempting to avoid errors altogether."

"If I could take myself back to how old you are now, I'd take action sooner. I wouldn't waste so much time worrying about 'what ifs'. I'd take more chances and correct as needed along the way. Because I now have absolute conviction that almost none of the things we worry about ever come to pass. And for anything that does go wrong, we handle it."

Your older, wiser self looks at you and smiles again. You sense immediately that she is completely unattached to the outcome. She hopes this knowledge shared inspires you, but she doesn't need *it to. Clearly, she has a trust in life and herself that you haven't yet. But her look tells you that's okay.*

In closing, she adds, "Get to know and trust your intuition. Believe in her. In time you will have much greater certainty. Until then, faith must be your conviction."

RELEASING

DROPPING THE WEIGHTS

I learned to scuba dive in the Red Sea, Egypt. But I almost didn't. I was progressing through the activities required for successful completion of my open water diving licence when I reached a breaking point and decided to quit.

I found the requirements challenging but I was getting through them, initially. I had successfully practiced losing my mask under the water and putting it back on again. I had also practised sharing a regulator in case I ever found myself without a working regulator. I didn't enjoy doing any of these kinds of activities, but it was necessary to persevere so that I could become a competent diver.

My breaking point came after the rescue swim. I don't remember the details exactly, but I think I had to swim about fifty metres, with all my scuba gear on, while pulling along my dive partner who was pretending to be unconscious. I completed the task, but just barely. I was exhausted.

I was also dismayed because within minutes of returning to the group, the instructor had us all lined up in the waist-deep water, ready to perform the next 'don't die diving' activity. We had to practise breathing with our regulators free-flow. This meant tilting my head sideways underwater, and then breathing in some of the air while the remaining free-flow air bubbles rose up to the surface.

I watched the instructor's demonstration of the exercise through my haze of exhaustion. I felt defeated. My spirit dropped and my heart sank as I realised I was done; I had to quit. Through tears of frustration, I told my instructor that I couldn't do it and stormed out of the water. On the beach, I took off all my scuba gear and found a place to console myself; I was never going to be a

diver. I was sad about it but, mostly, I was just glad to be out of a situation that was clearly not working for me.

Later, my instructor found me and tried to talk me into getting back in the water the next day. I resisted. "No, it's too much for me. I get anxious and exhausted. I'm just not strong enough and it's too hard." He looked thoughtful. "Just come back to the beach tomorrow and we'll work it out."

I went back reluctantly the next day. I couldn't see how the situation was going to improve. But I also really wanted to be able to dive. When I got to the beach, my instructor was holding a weight belt out to me. "I've removed half the weights. I think this might help."

Could it be that everything I'd been doing was unnecessarily hard because I had too many weights attached to me?

Yes. It turned out that one of the initial instructors had wrongly assessed the number of weights I'd need. With the excess removed, all my experiences in the water felt very different. It was easier to move, swim and complete any of the challenges the instructor set for me. I achieved my dive license and went on to have amazing dive trips in the years following.

It's how life works too. Many of us carry around very heavy pasts. We might have anger, frustration, betrayal or hurt, for example. These are all heavy and they weigh us down. They prevent us from moving easily and effectively in the present and into the future.

If we drop the weights we don't need, the present becomes easier and the future opens up in ways it could not have done otherwise.

KYLIE ZEAL

THOUGHTS HAVE WEIGHT

Dear Sister, do you ever wonder about the weight of your thoughts?

They have weight, you know; some more than others.

Some are heavy. They weigh you down and make it hard to move. The weight can make it challenging to even get started in the morning. And the energy required to keep moving while carrying around heavy thoughts can leave you feeling exhausted.

Heavy thoughts can't be seen on any scale. But you can feel their heaviness weighing on you. You feel them on your shoulders. On your head. On your heart. Not being able to see them can make things tricky; it can make you doubt their ability to impact you so much. But the weight you feel is all the evidence you need to know that these thoughts are preventing you from being confident and empowered.

Other kinds of thoughts are buoyant. They lift you up. You can grab onto those thoughts and feel yourself rise above life's challenges. The lighter they are, the higher you go, until you have a bird's eye view – just the perspective you need to get the big picture and a full understanding of what's really happening. You can see where you are now, where you want to be, and the path that will take you there.

Buoyant thoughts are what you need when inevitably, the unexpected happens. Life can and does change at any moment. One minute you're cruising through life, like a skipper on a boat. The next moment, you're thrown overboard. Perhaps the winds changed, or the seas got rough. Whatever the reason, you've found yourself splashing around, desperately thinking about how you can get back on the boat.

In those moments, more than ever, you need things that are going to help you float. You need thoughts that will assist you to gain clarity about how to deal with your challenges most effectively. You don't want to be drowning because you're attached to thoughts that weigh you down.

In those challenging times, you also need the people who are going to help you with buoyancy. When you look up at the boat, you'll see all the people who are scrambling to throw something to you. Some are going to throw you a life vest or life buoy of some kind. These are the people who will go out of their way to say words that help you rise above challenges and find the inner strength to keep going.

Unfortunately, even when you are paddling for your life, some people are going to throw weights at you. They may be well intentioned. Or they might be driven by fear and insecurity. Regardless, it's up to you to ensure you don't attach yourself to thoughts, people or things that weigh you down.

How much do your thoughts weigh, Sister? Do you need to let some thoughts or people go?

Some of your most valuable insights will come from simply noticing the weight. Some of your most effective moves will come from dropping the weights and seeing your life from a better, lighter, vantage point.

EMOTIONAL BAGGAGE REMOVAL

About every two or three months, the manager of my apartment building puts a notice up in the elevators to let everyone know that hard rubbish collection day is happening soon. Last time it happened, it was an opportunity for me to get rid of my broken toaster and my old desk. It's a great service that helps me remove unneeded belongings in a responsible way and make space in my home.

While it's annoying having to get the unwanted belongings down to the ground floor and outside to the collection point, I am really grateful that I don't have to do anything more than that. Who knows how long that old desk would have stayed in my apartment without this service?

Once the useless stuff is gone, I love the feeling of the space left behind. That space is called 'opportunity'. I can fill it with anything I want, or simply enjoy the clear space.

This process had me thinking about a service we could all use. Let's call it 'emotional baggage collection day'. Oh the space and 'opportunity' I'd have if my emotional baggage was collected and taken away, never to be seen again! I could fill the newly cleared out space inside me with anything I wanted. I could use the energy that used to go into managing all that baggage to create, to write, to form new relationships, or to solve problems. Or I could just bask in the peace that exists in that space.

In reality, of course, it's not possible to simply leave my emotional baggage at the door and have someone else do the work of taking it away. Nope, that's something I need to take care of myself. And I absolutely do need to take care of it because emotional baggage is an energy drainer and a breeding ground for self-sabotage.

I need to find the old, negative emotions no longer serving a purpose. This is different from emotions I experience in the present moment; they are providing me with important and useful information about my current situation. Those are messages I may need to heed for good decision making. But emotions about something that happened a day or a week ago or longer, that do not serve to make the present better, have got to go. That stuff is like out of date milk; it's rotten and it'll make you sick. Imagine milk that's been sitting in the fridge for a decade! Emotional baggage that's been held onto for that long is just as toxic.

Typical types of emotional baggage are resentment and anger. Guilt is also quite common. And hatred is a particularly rancid one. I need to, as a first step, find all these kinds of baggage within me, name them for what they are, and acknowledge that I've been carrying them around to no one's detriment but my own.

Then I need to let go. That's the second step. I know this can be easier said than done, but stay with me because there's no healthy reason to continue holding on. Carrying around that crap doesn't bring other people to justice or make them sorry. If they are sorry for the ways in which I believe they have wronged me, they are sorry regardless. Holding on to resentment won't make any difference to their level of remorse.

Still, we hold on to our emotional baggage as though it protects us. We think we need it as a reminder about what someone has done to us. As though it will guard us from that person in the future. Or help us be on the lookout for other people who might try to do the same.

There is some method in the madness but, mostly, it's just madness. All of the possible benefits of emotional baggage are minute compared to the freedom, empowerment and opportunity that is created by letting it go. Plus, we can still make smart decisions about other people, and who to let into our lives, without needing to protect ourselves with a layer of emotional baggage.

Letting go often requires forgiveness. I need to forgive – for real. That means one hundred percent, absolutely, no exceptions, removing that person or persons, and the memory of what they did, out of my mental space. Forgiveness is the spiritual version of the nice people who come to collect the hard rubbish from my apartment building.

This doesn't mean what happened was okay. Nor does it mean that person should stay in my life. It means I understand that I can't change the past. It means I have the energy to make smart decisions about the future based in self-worth and self-respect. It means I inhale and exhale deeply because I have removed the weight of emotional baggage.

For my own benefit, I need to forgive. I need to give myself the apology I am never going to get from the person who owes it. That's a bad debt that needs to be written off. I need to cut my losses and move on with my vision for my life.

I need to forgive even though it's not easy. Gandhi was one of the most forgiving and loving people who ever lived and he said, "The weak can never forgive. Forgiveness is an attribute of the strong."

It is an attribute of the strong... and the happy.

I forgive because I want to be happy.

FORGIVE

Dear Sister, one the most powerful abilities you have is forgiveness. It frees up energy for creating yourself and the life you want.

Feelings like anger, hurt, resentment, frustration and envy, as long as they are allowed to roam freely in your mind, are energy draining and distracting. They are like a mosquito buzzing around you in the dark. All you hear in the silence is the buzzing. That creature, while it may not seem like much, has the capacity to completely ruin your peace and rest. You need to get up and remove it in order to find your peace.

Forgiveness doesn't necessarily mean forgetting. It doesn't mean you weren't wronged, or that amends are not required. Nor does it mean a relationship must continue if that's not what you want.

Forgiveness means you are letting go of the resentment and negative energy that's interrupting your peace and blocking the channel to your inner wisdom.

DANCE ON THE ASHES

ANY IDIOT CAN FALL IN LOVE

Falling in love is like kicking a toe. It is not an act of will. It is something that just happens. Any idiot could do it.

Depending on how hard you fall, the experience can leave you not quite functional. I once kicked my foot on the base of my bed so hard that it broke (my toe, not the bed). I was lucky the weather was warm because the only shoes I could wear for a few weeks were flip-flops. Similarly, the experience of falling in love has left me severely impacted at different times in my life.

Falling in love is different to 'real love'. Real love is an act of will. As described by author M. Scott Peck in *The Road Less Travelled*, real love is 'the will to extend oneself for the purpose of nurturing one's own or another's spiritual growth.'

Peck further explains that to understand the experience of falling in love, it is necessary to know about ego boundaries. A newborn infant does not distinguish itself from the universe. When the infant moves its arms and legs, the world is moving. It cannot distinguish itself from the room, the world, and its parents. It and the world are one. Therefore, we say the infant has no ego boundaries.

In time, the child begins to experience itself as a separate entity. When it is hungry, mother or father doesn't always appear to feed it. When the child wants to play, there may be no-one available to play with. The child experiences its will as something separate from the behaviour of others. With age, ego boundaries continue to be defined, and by adolescence, people know they are individuals. Being able to maintain ego boundaries is healthy, while, at the same time, most people sense the aloneness associated with the separation. Until they fall in love…

Falling in love is the sudden collapse of a section of ego boundaries, permitting us to merge with another person. Suddenly loneliness is over and I will forever have this person who understands me! The connection is powerful and each person feels like they were made for the other. From one perspective at least, falling in love is an act of regression. We re-experience the sense of omnipotence we took for granted as young children.

Anthropologist and expert on romantic love, Helen Fisher calls romantic love a basic mating drive. It's a need, like hunger and thirst, that feels impossible to stamp out. Romantic love can be like an obsession or addiction and, when studying the brain activity of people in love, we can see similar brain activity as when looking at other kinds of addiction. Fisher says, 'We are not an animal that was built to be happy; we were built to reproduce.'

Damn biology and genes overriding my ability to make rational decisions! Over time, I feel I've had to become much more of a realist when it comes to romantic love. I have learned the hard way the importance of ensuring the love and respect I feel for myself is never exceeded by the value I place on another. To be out of balance in this area does not serve the other person and it undermines me and my ability to live effectively.

Have I become a cynic about romantic love? I sometimes wonder. I think my realism includes a healthy dose of scepticism but, ultimately, I'm a romantic. I believe romantic love is fuel for living an engaging, inspired and fun life. Love makes the heart sing and the soul dance. The experience of falling in love has been translated into songs and poetry and art. And romantic love doesn't have to fade, as is often suggested by the real cynics. But it does need to evolve into something greater.

I've learned I sometimes need to take a step back from the passion of romantic love and realise that it can cause more anguish than is necessary in everyday life. Without a level head and the mental capacity to rise above circumstances, romantic love creates more confusion, sadness, longing and frustration than necessary. Through my work, I've encountered many people whose lives have largely gone into paralysis because of romantic love.

Virtually no one gets through life without having been scathed by love. Nor is it the goal of life to get through scar free. The experience of having lost love is part of evolving a profound respect for real love and the discipline that is required to create it.

I am a body grounded in a human experience and with this comes biological drives and needs. I am also a soul capable of spiritual and emotional expansion – a soul that knows no ego boundaries and has no fear. Accepting I'm forever walking the line between these two realities will help me avoid being too much of an idiot when around those who leave me a little weak at the knees.

THERE IS A HAPPILY EVER AFTER

Dear Sister, the experience of falling in love is part of growing and evolving into the best version of you.

Embrace the fall.

Embrace it with a sense of balance between allowing yourself to free-fall into love and keeping your eyes open.

You'll see (if you keep your eyes open), love is as love does. Actions will always speak louder than words. Integrity is sexy.

Embrace falling in love with balance between showering your beloved with affection and standing firm in your self-love and self-worth.

You'll see (from self-worth as your highest vantage point), someone else's love is only a necessity when you aren't already filled with sufficient self-love. When you are filled, you are free to receive from open desire, rather than self-oppressed need.

Embrace falling in love with balance between holding on tight to the one you love and surrendering to complete faith that if it's meant to be, it will.

You'll see (from experience as your best teacher), anyone who is meant to be with you will be. And there are many different people who could be 'the one'.

Romeo and Juliet was a beautiful story of two people who placed romantic love above all else. But it ended tragically for four key reasons:

1. Poor communication skills
2. Making false assumptions
3. Believing they couldn't live without the love of their beloved.
4. They were teenagers who hadn't yet experienced enough about life to understand points 1–3 above.

If you enjoy romantic movies, don't stop enjoying them. Through actors on a screen, you can allow yourself to be completely drawn *into the drama, comedy and suspense. You can enjoy the way the characters grapple with themselves and their feelings for each other. Then, at the end, they finally see the truth of their love for each other in a scene that implies they now live happily ever after. Watching a movie like that is relaxing and heart-warming.*

Don't however let these movies get in the way of understanding, if the movie were to continue for another sixty-five years, it would be filled with more challenges than 'happily ever after' moments. By virtue of choosing to spend your life in relationship with another person, you are choosing to constantly navigate the reality of two people who rarely want exactly the same thing.

Dear Sister, do not interpret these words as cynicism about love. The intention is simply to leave unnecessary drama behind. Your time and energy are better channelled into the work of real *love. Into the courage to own your flaws, live authentically and sit with pain when it's present. Into cultivating your own happiness rather than expecting your partner to be responsible for it. Into learning how extraordinary you are. And into being the best version of yourself – someone capable of real love.*

The desire to love is not love. Love is courageous action for ourselves or others. Love is joy based in discipline. Love is the work of spiritual growth – and it doesn't get any better than spiritual growth.

With spiritual growth you find, perhaps ironically, there actually is a happily ever after.

LET IT BURN

Life is meant to change and evolve, and us with it. However, I'm not always willing to go along with the change. Many times, I have resisted the endings brought about by change. I have tried to cling to those things that have repeatedly revealed their desire to go. I have actively sought to hold on, thinking if I can just hold on for a bit longer, things will work out. If things do work out, then I have escaped the pain.

Letting go is painful. I know when I consent to the ending, some part of me must die too. By yielding, I am immersing myself in uncertainty – not only about the future, but about my ability to handle the wilderness.

It takes courage to hear the call to let go and then walk into the fire – the heat of the pain. It takes discipline and grit to let it burn, rather than retreat to the familiar. It burns and burns, sucking the oxygen right out of me. When it's over, I look around my life, exhausted and uncertain where to start. Wondering if I have what it takes to begin again.

But, ah, it has already begun. The space which looks barren and lifeless is already fertile ground. For it is immediately after the fire has raged through the forest, painting it black, that life begins again. It may not be visually apparent yet, but have faith. The rains will come and the sun will shine and life will sprout from the blackness in a way that leaves all witnesses struck by the audaciousness of it; that it would dare to rise up in spite of death.

DANCE ON THE ASHES

YOU WERE BORN FOR CHANGE

Dear Sister, life means change. Always, life will continue to change and it will keep taking you with it.

You can either go willingly, breathing it all in and transforming in the process. Or you can resist, kicking and screaming, until life finally drops you at your next destination, frustrated and disoriented because you spent much of the journey with your eyes closed.

You have the choice. Probably, you've done both. There were times you embraced the change with courage and grace. And there have been times you did all you could to avoid, prevent or resist the change.

Regardless of how you chose to take the journey, and whether the ending was welcome or painful, you eventually came to the same realisation: You cannot look forward and backward at the same time.

You cannot embrace the future while holding onto the past.

You cannot realise your potential while resisting your true nature, Sister. You were born for change.

SOME DAYS

Some days, like at the time of writing this, it all just seems a bit too much. I've been out all day. It was non-stop meetings and phone calls and a to-do list that was longer at the end of the day than it was at the beginning. The email inbox was the same. I know, logically, I have so much to be grateful for and, yet, I found very little joy in the events of today.

I could write about how 'I have first world problems', because that's what they are. And I often use that line to give myself perspective. Most days, it works. Most days start and end with a sense of gratitude. But this is not one of those days. I have gratitude in my head. Logically, I know how blessed I am. But I don't feel it in my body. I feel like, 'What's the point?' I feel sad about the world. I considered feeling pissed off about it, but I can't be bothered. I don't have the energy for that.

What the hell is everyone doing anyway? We're born, we fumble our way to adulthood and we pretend to be grown up until we work out what's going on, only to realise the grown-ups don't really know what they're doing either. We spend much of our lives scrambling around, trying to avoid pain or find joy. Then we get near the end and realise we're running out of time, and wish we'd spent less of our precious hours seeking external approval.

In this moment, I am more conscious of my current mood than I might be otherwise because I'm writing about it. I'm also aware of feeling embarrassed for my future 'self' who might actually publish these words and subject them to the judgement of readers. 'What a self-indulgent, depressive bore' are the judgements I imagine. And yet, right now, I'm too tired to even care about that.

I knew this day would come because it always does, even if only occasionally. Perhaps 'occasionally' is a blessing. Perhaps feeling this way for many days is known as depression. Or perhaps not. Either way, right now, in the middle of the darkness, I feel empathy for anyone who experiences this a lot.

I don't know for sure what causes it. Perhaps it's hormones. Perhaps it's just that I'm exhausted because I've been doing a lot physically, mentally and emotionally. Perhaps it's what I ate, or didn't eat. Perhaps it's loneliness. Perhaps it's helplessness, feeling like nothing I do will make a difference. Perhaps it's fear. Perhaps it's rage. I read somewhere 'depression is rage spread thin'. While I don't have depression, I wonder about this notion of rage spread thin. I can see the self-sacrifice of someone who would choose to turn their rage inward rather than lash out at the world. It's not the healthiest option but until better coping strategies are learned, I can see a level of responsibility being taken on by someone who would turn inward rather than be a burden to others. Perhaps this mood is a whole mixture of low-energy, hormones, helplessness, fear and rage.

Basically – and probably obvious from the number of times I've used the word 'perhaps' – I don't really know the cause of this mood I'm currently in the middle of. What I do know is overanalysing it is not going to alleviate it. I've also learned from my own experience that it won't last. The odds are very good that if I go to sleep soon and get a decent rest, I will feel at least fifty percent better in the morning. Sometimes, I wake feeling completely refreshed. Occasionally, it takes more than a day or two to pass. But it always passes.

Until it passes, I manage it best in several ways. First, I remind myself it will pass. Because everything does. Bad things pass. Good things pass. There's no need for me to get too caught up in any of it. I don't get too caught up in the high of a good day and think suddenly life is going to be great all the time (that's a recipe for disappointment). And I especially don't get too caught up in the bad days. They are absolutely not evidence that life will continue to be bad from now on.

Second, I continue to remind myself I'm doing well and there is nothing wrong with me. A low mood is not in any way a sign of failing. A low mood is simply a low mood and it doesn't mean anything unless I say it does. If my intuition tells me there is something more to my mood, perhaps something wrong, then I attend to that. I'll go see a health specialist, for example. But I never tell myself, or let anyone else dictate, that a mood means I'm in some way inadequate.

Third, I release 'expectations' from other people, society and myself. People can't help but place expectations on us, reasonable or not. We do the same to ourselves and others. Removing the need to meet expectations creates space for me to ask, 'What does my soul need right now?' and be able to hear the answer.

Eventually, I will face the world again and give it my best. Until then, a mood is just a mood and it will pass when it passes.

A CODE OF CONDUCT

Dear Sister, sometimes, life is hard. Often, even. You keep moving anyway, in spite of the weight, the demands, the no-end-in-sight. Despite no guarantee of reward, or even compensation, you keep moving.

You wonder if you are strong enough to meet all the challenges and sometimes, or often, don't know the answer to that question. What you do know is you don't necessarily require water to feel like you're drowning.

Sometimes, instead of rescuing yourself, you add 'poor swimming skills' to your long list of failings. You want to stop. You want to get out of the water. But there are people depending on you. It's one thing to let yourself down. It's worse to feel you've let down those counting on you. But something's got to give.

You're so close. So close to making a public announcement: "I have no idea what the fuck I'm doing! All the things that you think I am, I'm not. Somebody else take over because if I am left to be responsible, you're all going down with me."

Sister, when you get to this point, stop. It's time for you and your soul to regroup and come up with a new game plan. It's time for a good night's sleep. It's time for forgiveness. It's time for a healthy meal. It's time give your soul what she most needs and desires. It's time for release.

Release expectations and know that, when it comes to your life, you are a trailblazer. No-one has ever travelled exactly the same path as you. And for you to effectively navigate the trail every day, for the benefit of everyone, you need to be the healthiest you can.

Self-care is not an extravagance. Nor an indulgence. Or slacking off.

It is a necessity. A discipline. A code of conduct that must be adhered to.

THE SWEET SPOT

There is a sweet spot between guilt and resentment. I learned this while listening to Mario Martinez's book *The Mind Body Code*. Basically, Martinez instructs you to feel for emotions within your body. If you feel guilt, then you're probably not giving or doing enough. If you feel resentment, then you're probably giving or doing too much. The right amount of giving is the balance between these two feelings.

I'd never heard it described this way before, but I immediately knew exactly the internal place of peace he was referring to. I had discovered this place in the last couple of years, since becoming much better at saying 'no' to those things I didn't want.

At the same time as appreciating this powerful insight, I could see a problem with it: women rarely stop feeling guilty. Most of us, most of the time, are thinking about what more we could or should be doing. It's a thought process that has been ingrained in us by a culture that categorises women as nurturers and expects us to behave accordingly. And if we don't already feel guilty about the ways we are not meeting these expectations, we can be sure we'll receive feedback from somewhere in the culture determined to have us fulfil our role.

I'm now better at saying 'no', although it's not been easy to reach this point. And though I know the sweet spot Martinez is referring to, it often still eludes me.

I recently had an experience with someone who did not want to take 'no' for an answer. I continually had to stand my ground and maintain my boundaries, and I found it very challenging. I did not want to remove this person from my life altogether, but I found myself considering it several times, especially when trusted friends suggested I should.

This friend, who we'll call Kim, wanted more of my time and energy than I wanted to give. It seemed that no matter how much I gave, she always wanted more. I was an important part of her support network and it was important for me to be there for her up to a point. Unfortunately, the amount of help she requested constantly went beyond that point and I'd feel resentful. So I said 'no'.

She made her requests another couple of times in different ways. I repeatedly said 'no', believing that learning to resolve her own issues was ultimately what she needed anyway. She asked a few more times, using words that seemed designed to incite guilt in me, and I said 'no' one last time. Then after a disrespectful outburst from Kim, I decided to end communication for the foreseeable future.

I've long believed that I teach people how to treat me and if Kim was continuing to treat me like this, then I had played a role in that dynamic. I was determined to create new behaviour and results, and if Kim didn't like it, she had the choice to go find new friends who were willing to put up with her constant neediness and disrespect.

This was not easy for me. In spite of the fact that Kim was a grown woman and had demonstrated many times in the past that she was fully capable of looking after herself, she also seemed unstable and I feared she might self-harm. But I also knew that my constantly being there to fix her mistakes was not what she needed. If it was, then the issues would have been resolved by all the previous times that I had picked up the pieces for her. It seemed the change that most needed to happen was Kim taking full responsibility for her life, rather than me stepping in to rescue her.

Unfortunately, things got worse before they got better. When Kim called a few days later, I reluctantly answered the phone and learned that she had both self-sabotaged and self-harmed with alcohol and other means of escaping her reality. In the light of day, she expressed her disappointment in having treated herself and me so poorly and vowed to behave more maturely in future.

It all sounded positive until she began expressing her disappointment at how I, her friend, had not been there for her when she needed me the most. I respectfully but very firmly told her why I didn't agree and ended the call.

After I'd hung up the phone, I felt very curious. Something was missing. I mentally scanned my mind and my body and then realised what it was. I had no guilt.

I felt relieved that my friend was okay. And I was guilt-free.

I sat with the unusual feeling and explored it: *Of course I shouldn't feel guilty. I regularly give to many people in my life and it's reasonable for me to stop giving when it impacts negatively on my own life and wellbeing. If I believe I have reached the point where I need to reinforce my boundaries because they are being disregarded and disrespected, I can do that without guilt.*

Then, in the moment when I should have been basking in my empowerment and celebrating that perhaps I'd finally learned to value myself and respect my boundaries, something even more interesting happened… the voice of doubt crept in. That never-good-enough-no-matter-what-you-do voice in my mind rained on my empowerment parade: *Well, obviously you're a psychopath. Only psychopaths are without emotions. How could any normal, sane person not feel guilty after a friend self-sabotages and self-harms?*

I didn't know whether to laugh or get mad at myself. This guilt thing was relentless. *Am I not finally empowered and valuing myself, my life and my time? Can I not live my life without drama and guilt? Are you kidding me? A psychopath? Obviously, I'm not a psychopath or I wouldn't be having this conversation with myself. If I were a psychopath, I wouldn't even care about being a psychopath. Oh my goodness, does this never end?*

I stopped and laughed to myself. I could really drive myself mad with all this fearful self-talk! I wonder if Mr Martinez's head goes into this kind of a spin when he's feeling for the balance point between guilt and resentment. Or is it just me and my female friends with a high threshold for guilt?

KYLIE ZEAL

YOUR NORTH STAR

Dear Sister, your strengths are your weaknesses and vice-versa. What may be an incredible strength in one area of your life, might be your downfall in another.

If you are prone to guilt, know it is a strength that you care deeply. If you're a consistently high achiever, you're likely also familiar with self-criticism.

If you tend to be loud, know as a strength your ability to find a voice when others often cannot. If you are prone to introversion, you're likely also a very good listener.

You could suppose there is a balance in there somewhere. Between caring and guilt. Between speaking and listening. Between eating and fasting. Between reaching out and drawing back. Between exertion and relaxation.

There is always an optimal balance point, albeit elusive. It is a forever moving target.

Change any one of innumerable variables and the balance point shifts. What was once optimal is not any more.

Sometimes being off balance is desirable. Sometimes what's required is consciously veering off balance and being able to pivot when needed.

It's admirable to seek for the balance point; to take responsibility for finding it. But it is futile to criticise yourself or another for not achieving the balance point, let alone maintaining it for longer than five minutes.

Allow yourself the freedom to move, change and reassess. Error is inevitable in the life of a growing, striving and thriving human. So error-correction is a far more valuable skill than attaining perfection will ever be.

The perfect balance point is something you set your needle to and keep moving toward, even though you're not going to get there.

Like mastery or enlightenment or your potential, you won't ever achieve them, not completely. Rather, your role is to ensure you're facing toward them.

They are your north star.

RISING

C.L.E.A.R. THINKING

My work, ultimately, is about helping people become C.L.E.A.R. thinkers. When someone is adept at C.L.E.A.R. (Creative, Logical, Empathetic, Agile, Resourceful) thinking, life is better. And that's what people who seek me out are looking for – a better life. A more effective, healthier, happier life.

Most often, the people who contact me are women who are already doing a lot of things well. They're smart, driven and have already taken some adventures outside of their comfort zone. But they're also tired of being tired. Sometimes they're completely overwhelmed by their to-do lists. They would like life to be better without doing 'more'. Though they haven't yet worked out how, they believe it's possible to achieve more without spending extra time and energy. And they're right.

Like my client, Bec, for example. She'd already been running her business for around five years when she contacted me. She'd heard about me from another client and was interested in creating similar changes, i.e. increased leadership capabilities, working fewer hours per week and a more profitable business.

Within three months Bec was taking the actions that she'd been thinking about taking for years, including signing a lease for larger business premises and hiring new staff. What was most exciting was thinking about all the people her business would be able to serve and how she would be able to contribute even more to her family (including spending more time with her young kids) through running an effective, successful, conscious business.

One of the most important things Bec and I did together was raise her thinking above her fear. Fear is always present when you're stretching yourself and outside your comfort zone. You can't escape it. But you can rise above it.

When you raise your consciousness above your fear, you become C.L.E.A.R. in your thinking and that means you are:

Creative – Without fear in the way, you are more creative, innovative and inspired. You think of new ways to generate income or fun ways to incorporate exercise into your day. You find creative answers to problems, and more efficient ways to achieve the results you want.

Logical – When the voice of fear isn't catastrophising all the things that could go wrong, suddenly what's possible and the way forward seems logical. With logic, you can recall that you have survived 100 percent of your worst days and you're wiser now for having gone through those experiences. You also logically see you're competent enough to handle future challenges, whatever they may be. It might not be easy, but you have the smarts to find a way.

Empathetic – Fear tends to make us suspicious of other people's motives. It causes us to distrust and that can lead to breakdown in relationships, whether with your spouse, colleagues, staff or friends. In Bec's case, her negotiations for her new lease went much more smoothly when she was able to see the situation from the agents perspective and not take anything they said personally. This in turn gave her the confidence to ask for exactly what she wanted.

Agile – Change is inevitable. The unexpected will happen and you will make mistakes. When your thinking sits above your fear, you're more agile and can move with changes (unexpected or not) and pivot if needed, without losing sight of your overall goal. You keep take action rather than becoming stalled when changes happen.

Resourceful – From above your fear you can see where your resources are. Whether it's drawing on strength and wisdom within you, engaging the right specialist for the challenge at hand, or calling on a friend, your resourcefulness helps you see options and multiple solutions to any problem.

To a large extent, creativity, logic, empathy, agility and resourcefulness exist within you already. But you can't always access them because of fear getting in the way, keeping you in lower level thinking. When you remove unnecessary fear and raise your consciousness, C.L.E.A.R. thinking happens quite naturally.

REVEAL

Dear Sister, the most beautiful outfit you will ever wear is confidence.

So remove your overcoat. Take off that heavy layer of self-doubt and fear. And drop your stories about why you're not good enough.

You think it's cold out, and you need protection. But you'll find, when you remove the cloak, you radiate. And your beauty will warm up the space around you.

Your task is not to create an empowered woman.

All you need do is reveal her.

SILENCE IS MY HUSTLE

The fastest way to the things I want, ironically, is to slow down. I've learnt that slowing down allows me to raise my consciousness, think clearly and, ultimately, forge a more direct path to the things I want. To the life I want.

But slowing down can be hard! With the way the world functions, if I try to slow down, I am swimming against the current, surrounded by fearful voices yelling, "If you slow down, you're going to get left behind!"

The temptation to keep busy is strong. The need to keep up with everybody's social media happy snaps is pervasive. When I do, finally, make time to slow down, the silence, if I haven't been there for a while, is uncomfortable at best. Immediately, I'm tempted to escape the silence by tuning into the latest series that can be streamed via the Internet with the push of a button. The entertainment gives me a break from all the external noise and an escape from the chatter in my head. Without the distraction, silence and I sit side by side awkwardly, like two people who have just met and don't know what to talk about. When I'm at that stage, I know I've got some work to do in order to rebuild my mental muscles.

You could say 'silence is my hustle'. When the path of least resistance is 'busyness' because that's the norm for much of society, then attempting to move in a different direction takes strength, patience and focus. It takes hustle to find a place where my mind is calm and clear and I can hear my inner wisdom. But it's worth the effort because it really is the most significant thing I can do for effective living. My inner wisdom is far too important to be missed simply because I didn't make time for silence.

In silence, there is no worry or fear. There is no scarcity. There is clarity.

In silence exists infinite possibilities. The answer to every question. The solution to every problem.

In silence I can hear my soul's wisdom. And the soul always knows what to do for my highest good.

The soul also knows everything is going to be okay. Hence, it's an important source of courage.

And the soul is always present. It's just not very loud. At least it's not louder than the mind (where worry and fear are located).

So, this is the objective: Silence the mind. Silence the constant stream of chatter and find my truth, courage and wisdom.

BE SILENCE

Dear Sister, the quieter you become, the louder and clearer you'll hear your truth. It's the sweetest irony – go quiet to become louder.

Create a habit worthy of your life: Start your day with silence.

Even if it's only a few minutes, take time for this important ritual. Clarity in the morning can determine the course of your entire day.

We do not lack time so much as we lack direction. We do not lack love, but we tend to forget it in the noise and the busyness of life.

Go into silence to remind yourself of all that is most important to you. 'Be silence' and find the answers you seek already there, waiting for you in the still spaces within you.

The world needs you on your terms. But what are your terms? Where are your boundaries? What are you a 'no' to? And what are you a 'yes' to?

Your answers are in the silence.

What would you do if the only voice you felt compelled to listen to was yours? Not the voice of a fearful mind. Not the voice that echoes external noise. But your wise, brave, sweet yet no-nonsense inner voice that lives in the silence.

IT LOOKS THE SAME BUT IT'S ACTUALLY DIFFERENT

"I can't believe we have to deal with this again."

These are my client's words, though they may as well be mine. I know that feeling. I know that frustration. It's the feeling I get when I've done so much work on myself, and challenged myself over and over, and yet here I am again at the same crossroads. Here I am, once again, seemingly stalled in my progress because of my issues around self-worth and courage. Here I am, once again, questioning whether I have a right to go after the things I really want and for which I'm willing to work. Or questioning my right or ability to say 'no' to those things that I sense are not good for me.

I remind myself the same thing I tell my clients: It might look the same, but it's actually different.

My client, Laura, and I have been journeying together through coaching for more than five years, so when I say to her, "It's not the same", I know what I'm talking about. I remember where she was at when we first began coaching together. I know how much she has progressed and it is nothing short of amazing. And, yet, here we are, working on her latest goals, and things aren't progressing as she'd like.

We peel back the layers. We want to understand, when we go beneath all of the surface, symptomatic stuff, what's left. What's the core of the issue?

Finding the answer takes discussion prompted by some thought-provoking questions. We explore what's been happening, how Laura has been responding, and what exactly she has been telling herself (her self-talk or inner chatter.)

Then we arrive at our destination, the place where there is no more illusion, only the undeniable truth: She is undervaluing herself. Her self-talk is some variant of "I'm not good enough."

Almost as soon as she sees this truth, Laura makes two errors.

First, she makes the mistake of thinking it's exactly the same issue we've covered in the past.

Second, she berates herself for not having yet mastered the lesson she believes we have gone over many, many times before. Additionally, she allows herself to feel embarrassed or ashamed because she imagines I must be judging her for not having graduated past this weakness yet.

I respond: It looks the same, but it's actually different.

This is probably true for everyone who is pursuing personal development, but I genuinely know it's true for Laura because

I've journeyed with her. For example, I know that three years ago, there were some important conversations Laura was not willing to have. But after several coaching sessions and with practice, she successfully had those conversations. Over time, she's had many of them. And, now, those conversations don't make her anxious. Having those conversations became 'just another thing she does'.

How swiftly she has forgotten the anxiety she used to feel at just the thought of those conversations. How quickly she has taken her hard-earned skills for granted.

Courageous became her new normal. Until the context changed.

She changed the context. She upped the ante when she allowed herself to imagine, even for a moment, she could do more. Be more.

Almost as soon as she had taken on her new, more courageous identity, her spirit was calling her forward again. Her intuition began whispering ever so gently, *This is what you were born for.*

So she again moved forward, into the unknown, into a new context. This time it was an interview for a role more senior than she'd ever done, at an organisation she dreamed of working for.

The new context was one in which she'd never been in before. And even though she had excellent, relevant skills, she'd never practiced them in this situation which felt high stakes to her. So now she finds herself, once again, fumbling her way around and fearing, at any moment, someone may find out. At least, this is what fear tells her.

Fear has known Laura all her life and knows exactly where she is most vulnerable. Fear knows precisely when to step in and what to say to strike a nerve. Fear, if allowed, would have Laura believe she hasn't really progressed at all for she carries the same weaknesses with her wherever she goes.

But I know the truth. I understand the main reason Laura is feeling anxious is because she is venturing into new territory and this requires her to take her self-worth and courage up a level.

So I repeat, "It looks the same but it's actually different."

THE HIGHER YOU GO, THE BETTER THE VIEW

Dear Sister, you have journeyed a long way, mostly uphill.

Occasionally, or even many times on the journey, you have fallen. But for every time you got back up, for every step you continued to take in faith, you built muscles.

No step was wasted. Each was your becoming.

And look who you've become. Pause and really look, because so much of your awesomeness is taken for granted. Too often you undervalue your extraordinary gifts.

Your gifts and talents, intuition and wisdom are your awesomeness and they are ultimately all you need to get you where you're going. Nothing is missing.

You will continue to experience challenges as you journey. This has never changed and it won't change. It will still be uphill, much of it, and you will continue to carry the weight of your own self along the path. But, as you already know, the higher you go on your self-development journey, the better the view.

Look around. Notice how far you have travelled. It's extraordinary and you've earned all of it.

Now, look even further. See the horizon. See the path you've yet to tread and for which you are ready.

MY EDITOR WAS SO ANNOYING

The first time I submitted this book for editing, my editor did a structural edit, which means she moved a lot of things around. When I got the book back I wasn't sure how I felt about it. Part of me liked the changes, but another part just couldn't get on board with them. After sitting with it for a few days, I ended up changing a whole lot of content around so that it looked nothing like what either of us had previously done with the manuscript.

It left me wondering, "Why did I get the book edited if I was just going to go and change it all? Did I just waste all the money I invested in getting the manuscript edited?"

But no. I could see that my third version of the book (my favourite so far) would never have been created if my editor hadn't first made all those changes – I just wouldn't have seen the vision for the third version without being forced to see the second version; I was too attached to the first.

To her credit, my editor was quite brave to take my work and change it to the extent she did. I remember, at one point, being quite annoyed because I couldn't see the original version I'd invested so much time, energy and soul into.

But I also couldn't go back. I didn't want to go back. Amongst my frustration, I could see she was onto something. And the longer I sat with the idea of what my book was about, as well as a new perspective that my editor had enabled me to see, the more I began to see a new vision for the book.

Sometimes people do things we really don't want. It's especially annoying when they mess with our plans, or values, or force us outside of our comfort zone.

But if we can breathe through the discomfort and trust in our ability to work through any challenge, then we may find these annoying people become the catalyst for exactly the change we need.

We could also think of it like a game of tennis. You need more than one player if you're going to get any good at the game. You could hit the ball at a wall. That would help get your fitness up and improve your skills somewhat. But the improvement would be little compared to having someone else hitting the ball across a net toward you – especially if that person is better at the game than you.

LIFE'S WAY OF MAKING YOU BETTER

Dear Sister, whenever you think you're being rejected, you're actually being redirected to something better.

When life has you weak and fallen to the ground, there's something down there you're supposed to find.

Life can be difficult. Often frustrating. Painful too.

But keep going. Keep looking. Keep feeling.

Those things, people and events that challenge you are life's way of making you better. Stronger. Wiser.

MY TRIBE

A few years back, when I was new to my building, I met another resident who we'll call Natalie. I thought she was lovely. She had her issues, like the rest of us, but I enjoyed her company. We went walking after work several times. I invited her to my place once for dinner. She'd invited me to her birthday party the following month. Then she just disappeared. She stopped returning my calls and messages.

I find behaviour like this weird (though I know it's not uncommon). Moreover, it's rude, selfish and lacks integrity. If there is something I've done to upset you, then say it. And if you've decided we'll no longer be friends, then have the courtesy to not waste my time following up to check if you're okay. But people like Natalie don't do that because they're afraid of confrontation. Best case scenario, she believes she's saving my feelings from being hurt.

I'll likely never know why she did it. I've thought about pursuing that information from her, but then then I stop myself because I don't actually want people in my inner circle who behave that way. And though I believe there could be potential benefit in getting her feedback because there may be some aspect of my personality that could be improved upon, I already have friends who willingly give me honest and direct feedback. They aren't afraid to point out my good qualities, as well as my flaws.

Of course, Natalie's disappearing act may have nothing to do with me. But if it was because of something I did, odds are, whatever negative feedback Natalie has about me, I'm aware of it and I'm either working on it or made my peace with it. Plus, if she believes I don't know how to receive critical feedback with maturity, then how accurate can her feedback about me be anyway?

So, I let it go. Furthermore, I willingly let go of all the 'Natalies'. I wish them well and I give them full permission to opt out of my life. It frees up my energy for the people with whom I have similar values and a mutual connection.

At a recent birthday dinner I organised for myself, I sat in the middle of a long table in a private room at a local restaurant. Also at the table were ten women from my tribe. One I'd known for a while, but we'd only been close for about six months. Some, I'd known for a decade or more. One I'd known since I was a child.

The dinner was such an enjoyable, powerful experience. Once we were all seated, I went round the table and introduced each guest, letting all the other guests know how I'd met that person and something about them. After that, while glorious food was enjoyed by all, I had everyone at the table take turns in speaking about themselves and what they wanted to create in their life in the coming year. It was a powerful conversation with everyone listening intently to the speaker, occasionally offering compliments or tips.

The joy and positive feedback from my tribe at the end of the dinner was overwhelming. They loved meeting like-minded women and learning so much about everyone there, including those at the other end of the table who they'd likely have learned nothing about if we'd not conducted conversation that way. I loved it too because I was able to show genuine interest in and experience quality conversation with everyone there; they all meant a lot to me.

I'm so grateful for each and every one of the women in my inner circle. I'm also grateful to myself for fostering such powerful friendships. I stay connected, I'm genuinely interested in their happiness and success, and I love them. An important part of this is loving myself. When I do that, I show up to friendships, new and old, as my authentic self and attract people with similar values.

Being 'me' might mean people like Natalie choose to opt out of my life. That can be disappointing, but it's also very good, because they make room at my table for someone who's meant to be there.

EMPOWERED WOMEN EMPOWER WOMEN

Dear Sister, if you have the chance to gather with conscious women, especially if you haven't in a while, take it.

A circle of conscious women is so powerful. It is fertile ground for growth and healing. It's a perfect space for exploring new ideas, sharing your secrets and, above all, lots of laughs.

I like to gather. Circles of two women are common for me. Circles of three or more, and occasionally more than ten, are equally pleasing. The circle is an unencumbered space in which women can do what they do best – connect, nurture, inspire and create.

We would like to be equally unencumbered when males are around. We're getting better at that, but it can still be challenging, especially in public settings. As discussed in Sheryl Sandberg's book, **Lean In,** *from a very early age, boys are encouraged to take charge and offer their opinions. But when* *girls call out, teachers often scold them for breaking the rules and remind them to raise their hands if they want to speak.*

Sandberg goes on to say, "In time, the danger goes beyond authority figures silencing female voices. Young women internalise societal cues about what defines "appropriate" behaviour and, in turn, silence themselves." None of this is specifically the fault of 'men'. Rather, we live in a patriarchal system perpetuated by many men and women.

Your female connections are a source of strength and courage – both of which you need to help overcome barriers in the wider world. At least they should be a source of strength and courage. If they're not, they may not be your tribe. If your female friends attempt to disparage you, put a stop to it. And if you ever catch yourself behaving that way toward them, stop.

Empowered women empower women. It's that simple.

A conscious, empowered woman has a tribe of women who've got her back, and she's got theirs. They are like queens who fix each other's crowns.

I'd like to say, when women gather, 'magic' happens. While it might feel magical sometimes, the reality is, when we consciously gather, what happens is perfectly natural.

Find your bliss-filled tribe and love 'em hard. If you've found them, then you already know you've tapped into one of the greatest sources of courage, strength and love available to you.

AN UNDENIABLE MELODY

I used to buy into phrases like 'you're too emotional' or 'don't be so sensitive' in the way they were intended – as insults.

Repressing feelings was role modelled for me and, consequently, I tended to block out much of the important information and insights that my emotions provided me. At least, I tried to block them out, which lead to internal conflict between what I couldn't help feeling and the denial of what I was feeling.

Well, not anymore. I wised up.

Our emotions are intimately linked to our intuition. They are the most honest response to what we experience in each moment.

Our emotions are like the vinyl on the record player and our intuition is the needle. When we are willing to allow the two to connect, there is an undeniable melody. But, first, we must be willing to set the needle down and pull our fingers out of our ears so we can hear the music.

When we hear the music, the instinct is to dance. To stomp and sway and leap. To turn and jump and stretch. To move.

But then we hesitate. We fear failure, judgement or criticism. And fear is often louder than the music.

Which is curious because the music is real and the fear is not.

When we let go of fear, we dance.

COURAGEOUS AND OUTRAGEOUS

Dear Sister, whatever you came into this world for, whatever your soul calls you to, that's your dance.

When you take courageous action, when you respond to the truth you feel, that's your dance.

Some may criticise your dance. When they witness the divine feminine moving with freedom, it can make them uncomfortable. Feminine energy at its most free is unpredictable and can't be planned. It doesn't abide by rules about how to behave so others can feel comfortable. It feels truth and responds to what is happening now. It hears the music and feels the urge.

Others will be inspired. They're also tired of waiting for an invitation to the dance floor. When you take courageous action, you are a dance teacher. You are helping like-minded people find their rhythm.

Sister, go for courageous and outrageous. Find your spot on the floor and declare to yourself, or out loud, "Stand back, because I've got some moves. You can support me or you can leave. Either way, this is my floor and I'm here to dance."

WORKS CITED

Adamczyk, A. (2016, August 13). *Why Women Talk Less than Men at Work*. Retrieved 2017, from http://time.com/money/4450406/men-interrupt-talk-more/

Altman, L. (2012, March). *How Emotion Shapes Decision Making*. Retrieved July 2017, from https://intentionalworkplace.com/2012/03/15/how-emotion-shapes-decision-making/

Fisher, H. (2006, February). *TED*. Retrieved from www.ted.com: https://www.ted.com/talks/helen_fisher_tells_us_why_we_love_cheat

Gilligan, C. (2011). *Joining the Resistance* (Kindle Edition). Cambridge: Polity Press.

Peck, M. S. (1978). *The Road Less Traveled: A New Psychology of Love, Traditional Values and Spiritual Growth*. New York: Simon & Schuster.

Sandberg, S. (2013). *Lean In; Women, Work and the Will to Lead* (Kindle edition). New York: Alfred A. Knopf, a division of Random House.

UN Women. (n.d.). Retrieved June 2017, from http://www.unwomen.org/en/what-we-do/leadership-and-political-participation/facts-and-figures#notes

ACKNOWLEDGMENTS

To my coaching clients. You face your fears and take courageous action (your dance!). Thank you for all you do for yourself, for the greater good, and for inspiring me.

To my editors and proof readers: Jacqui Pretty and Sara Litchfield of the Grammar Factory, thank you so much for your insights and expertise on writing. Annette, Kate, Sarah, Khy, Janie, Madeleine, Dush and Caroline, your time, interest, encouragement and feedback were so much appreciated.

To my publishing team: Julia Kuris of Designerbility – Another great cover design. Thank you for your insights, expertise, creativity, professionalism and patience. Charlotte Gelin – Thank you for your excellent work on the internal design of the book. Kosta Iatrou of Ikon Images – You've captured so many great photos, including the one we put on the cover of this book!

Thank you to Avril for listening to me talk about the book every week and always being interested.

Thank you Glenn for every investment you made into me and this book.

Thank you to all my family and friends for believing in me.

Thank you to everyone who has supported me on my journey.

ABOUT THE AUTHOR

Kylie Zeal is a Professional Development Coach, certified by the International Coach Federation. She is passionate about helping women be confident and empowered.

Kylie spent two years managing a research project exploring the benefits of coaching. At the completion of the project, she facilitated coach training across Australia. Kylie has a bachelor of Social Science with majors in psychology and sociology.

Dance on the Ashes is her second book.

To learn more about Kylie Zeal and find out how you can follow on social media, go to www.kyliezeal.com

www.ingramcontent.com/pod-product-compliance
Lightning Source LLC
Chambersburg PA
CBHW030436010526
44118CB00011B/660